BUMP, SET, SPIKE!
EVERYBODY'S VOLLEYBALL BOOK

JOE PEDERSEN AND VICTOR LOGGINS

CONTEMPORARY
BOOKS, INC.
CHICAGO ▪ NEW YORK

Library of Congress Cataloging-in-Publication Data

Pedersen, Joe.
  Bump, set, spike!

  1. Volleyball.   I. Loggins, Victor.   II. Title.
GV1015.3.L64   1986   796.32'5   86-8824
ISBN 0-8092-5075-6

Photos by John Patrick Tueth, Tueth Visuals, Chicago

Copyright © 1986 by Joe Pedersen and Victor Loggins
All rights reserved
Published by Contemporary Books, Inc.
180 North Michigan Avenue, Chicago, Illinois 60601
Manufactured in the United States of America
Library of Congress Catalog Card Number: 86-8824
International Standard Book Number: 0-8092-5075-6

Published simultaneously in Canada by Beaverbooks, Ltd.
195 Allstate Parkway, Valleywood Business Park
Markham, Ontario L3R 4T8 Canada

CONTENTS

INTRODUCTION

VOLLEYBALL ORIGINS

William Morgan Invents a Game

Once upon a time, in the not so far away land of Holyoke, in the Commonwealth of Massachusetts, there was a man called William Morgan. He was the physical director of the Young Men's Christian Association, and he had a problem. In 1895 the most popular game in his gymnasium was basketball, and it was just too rigorous for some of his members who were middle-aged. Morgan wanted a game that would provide physical activity and exercise without being overly rigorous and taxing.

Morgan had no knowledge of any such game, so, with typical turn-of-the-century Yankee aplomb, he invented one. He decided to borrow rules and equipment from games already in existence. From tennis, Morgan took the net. He mounted it across half a basketball court at a height of six and a half feet. From a basketball he took the soft inside bladder to use as the ball in his game. He wanted a fairly soft ball that would not hurt or injure players hands. From baseball he took the concept of nine innings and three outs. From polo he took nothing, thank God.

Playing the game consisted of hitting the ball back and forth over the net. Techniques from tennis and handball were used. Morgan called his new game *mintonette*. Obviously not a very catchy name because by 1897, the name was changed to *volleyball.*

Of the original rules that Morgan initiated, the only ones still left in the game are:

1. The ball's dimensions are 25–27 inches in circumference.
2. A player hitting the net ends play.
3. The ball may not be caught or held.
4. Conduct is sportsmanlike. Conjecturing on the possible family lineage or sexual habits of the opponents, referee, or spectators is considered *déclassé* and will result in your expulsion from the game.

The YMCA Spreads the Game

For about the next 30 years, the YMCA controlled the game of volleyball. At the turn of the century, the Y was the only national organization with its own gym facilities. The YMCA updated the rules in 1912 and again in 1916, this time with the help of a small organization that called itself the National Collegiate Athletic Association. The first National YMCA Championship was held in Brooklyn, New York in 1922, and the Pittsburgh YMCA took home whatever it was they gave away for first place. Like most awards, it probably ended up on a shelf somewhere and was the topic of many boring conversations until it was thrown out because it was too much trouble to dust.

Because the YMCA never could just stay home and mind its own business, it had, by 1920, spread volleyball to Canada, the Orient, Cuba, Puerto Rico, Uruguay, Brazil, and the Philippines. The earliest foreign competition was held in Manila in 1913 at the Far Eastern Games.

Filipinos made another large contribution to volleyball in 1916. They developed an offensive attack in which one player would pass the ball in a very high trajectory to a second player who would jump into the air and hit the ball as hard as he could into the opponent's court. The player who hit the ball was called a *bomberino,* and the play itself was called a *bomba.* Now that's a catchy name.

The USVBA Is Born

In 1928 the United States Volleyball Association (USVBA) was born. Its dual purpose was to provide a framework for an open tournament and to bring uniformity to the rules. The USVBA divided the United States into geographical regions for the purpose of local participation and control. This philosophy of regional authority is still followed today.

Volleyball Catches On

Volleyball is a natural sport for outdoor play, and this form of the game began just after the turn of the century. Volleyball quickly gained popularity, especially with young people, who introduced their parents to the game. Before long, volleyball nets were being strung up at picnics, playgrounds, backyards, beaches, or anywhere people were interested in recreation and exercise. Recreational sports were becoming more important in American life as Americans had increasingly more time for recreation.

On the international scene, volleyball gained tremendous exposure via the greatest disseminator of cultural exchange the world has ever known—namely war. The doughboys of World War I did much to promote volleyball abroad. The American Expeditionary Force distributed over 15,000 volleyballs to our soldiers and to the Allied forces.

During the Second World War, the armed forces were again responsible for introducing large numbers of our citizen soldiers and foreign nationals to volleyball. Nothing draws a crowd faster than the sight of people competing in some sort of game. And, of course, today's spectator is tomorrow's participant.

There were two drawbacks to the exposure volleyball gained during the two world wars. First, there was insufficient time to teach the troops the rules of play; second, no upward limit was placed on the number of players on a side. As a result, Americans began to perceive volleyball as a unique but noncompetitive sport calling for a minimum of physical activity and coordination.

Meanwhile, in U.S.-occupied foreign countries, volleyball was growing along highly competitive lines. The game was still played for fun, but a high value was placed on strategy, team play, and sound fundamentals.

In 1964, under the sponsorship of the host nation, Japan, volleyball became an Olympic sport. Under the direction of the USVBA, American teams began competing in Olympic volleyball. Let's take a look at the results from Tokyo in 1964 to Montreal in 1976:

TOKYO, 1964

Men	Women
1. U.S.S.R.	Japan
2. Czechoslovakia	U.S.S.R.
3. Japan	Poland

MEXICO CITY, 1968

Men	Women
1. U.S.S.R.	U.S.S.R.
2. Japan	Japan
3. Czechoslovakia	Poland

MUNICH, 1972

Men	Women
1. Japan	U.S.S.R.
2. East Germany	Japan
3. U.S.S.R.	North Korea

MONTREAL, 1976

Men	Women
1. Poland	Japan
2. U.S.S.R.	U.S.S.R.
3. Cuba	Korea

MOSCOW, 1980

Men	Women
1. USSR	USSR
2. Bulgaria	W. Germany
3. Romania	Bulgaria

LOS ANGELES, 1984

Men	Women
1. U.S.A.	China
2. Brazil	U.S.A.

How could Americans do so poorly at a game of their own invention? Simple. Not enough people know the rules and play by them. That's what turns out athletes who excel in any sport: a wide basis of participation and a common knowledge of uniform rules.

William Morgan had wanted a game designed primarily for people who could not participate in strenuous activity. More adept athletes have changed that approach to the game, and gradually volleyball has evolved into its present Olympic form. But it still retains the original philosophy that the sport should be fun.

The United States Women's team in action.

VOLLEYBALL VARIATIONS

Volleyball can be played on more age and skill levels than possibly any other game. This popularity and widespread knowledge of the basic game have given birth to many different forms of playing it. The variations range from those which require only a modest athletic ability to those which demand a high degree of coordination, stamina, and skill. Among the variations are recreational volleyball, newcomb, four-person volleyball, wallyball, and doubles. Another variation, beach volleyball, is described in Chapter 8.

Recreational Volleyball

The regulation number of players on a side in competitive volleyball is six. However, in the United States volleyball is played informally. Nets are strung up in school yards, at family picnics, in public parks, and in forest preserves. The games played in these settings frequently include more than the regulation number of players and are played more for good times than physical benefit.

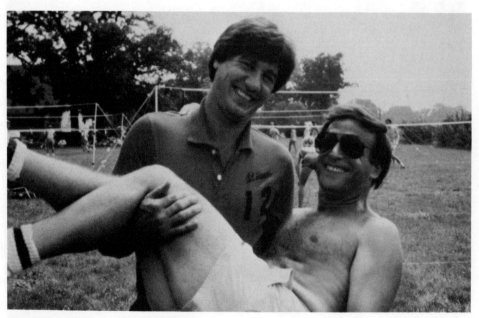

Two extremely recreational players.

Six players on a side may be ideal for covering the 30-by-30-foot area of the court. But there is absolutely nothing wrong with putting additional players on the court, so long as everyone understands that the game is being played for fun and not competitively. Indeed, in some situations, such as with very young students or with older people, it would be foolish *not* to play with nine, ten, or even more players on a side. The main ingredient in these games is the same as their object: *fun!*

Newcomb

Newcomb is volleyball without the volley. It is frequently taught to children in the fourth and fifth grades as an introduction to the basic concepts of volleyball. This type of game can also be enjoyed by enthusiatic adults who may have diminished athletic ability.

Depending on the age of the participants, newcomb should be played with at least nine on a side. The net may be lowered. Play is initiated by throwing the ball over the net from outside the back-court line. The ball must be caught and thrown back by a player on the other side. Points are scored when the ball falls to the floor, goes out of bounds, or is touched more than once on a side. The game is usually played to 15 points.

Once the players have mastered the basic game, variations can be employed to promote a more spirited workout and teach team effort. Allowing three touches on the same side of the net before the ball is returned encourages accurate and fast handling of the ball to score points. If a player drops the ball while passing it, the opponents score a point.

Four-Person Volleyball

There are several good reasons for playing with four people on a side. First, players are required to cover a larger than normal area on the court. This helps sharpen quickness and anticipation in each player. Second, there is a greater likelihood for an individual player to be actively involved in each volley than there is on a regulation-size team. For beginners trying to perfect their basic skills, or for those already proficient in those skills, this is ideal. A team member can reasonably expect to bump, set, spike, block, or use a combination of those skills on a single play.

Strategically, teams line up in a diamond formation to receive the serve *(see Figure 1)*. The player in the front of the diamond is

FIGURE 1: SERVE RECEPTION IN 4-PERSON VOLLEYBALL

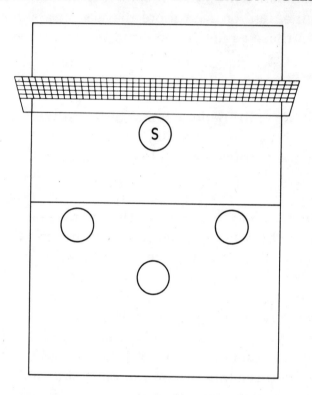

the designated setter; the player at the back of the diamond usually plays the back-court and stays deep. The players on either side come up to the net only to block or spike as the situation demands. Rotation is clockwise, and the serve area is the same as in the six-person game. This variation of volleyball develops good court sense, stamina, and self-confidence, and it provides strenuous competition. It is very fast-paced.

Wallyball

First conceived in 1979, wallyball is the latest craze in volleyball-related games. It is estimated that as many as half a million people currently participate in wallyball in over 2,500 health and racquetball clubs in this country.

As its name implies, wallyball is a cross between volleyball and racquetball. It can be played with as few as two persons on a side or as many as four. A volleyball net is simply strung across a racquetball court at a height of eight feet, and you're ready to play.

Wallyball begins with the serve, just as in volleyball. The server must stand outside the three-foot line on the racquetball court and may not cross or touch this line before the ball is struck. The serve may go directly over the net or carom off a wall before or after crossing the net. It may not hit more than one wall, and it may not hit the back wall at all. The receiving team may touch the ball three times before they must return it. When the ball is returned, it may be played off a wall, but the same prohibition applies to hitting the opponents' back wall. Only the serving team can score points. Points are scored, or a change of serve is forced, when the ball touches the floor, strikes an out-of-bounds wall, or is not returned after three touches. In general, the basic rules of volleyball prevail.

Games are played to 15 points, and the victor must win by two points. Regardless of the number of players on a side (two, three, or four), the players must rotate clockwise when the serve changes sides.

Wallyball is a unique and challenging game that depends on the strategies of racquetball and the ball-handling skills of volleyball. It provides a stimulating workout.

Doubles

What the *Grand Prix* is to auto racing, doubles play is to volleyball. Only the very best need apply. A player who passes poorly, sets inaccurately, or lacks stamina can expect an unmerciful beating—if not outright humiliation—when playing with only two on a side. There is no place to hide. Speed, anticipation, and accurate ball handling are needed just to keep the ball in play. Let's face it, you're trying to cover an area usually played by six people, not two. You'd better be good.

The general rules of volleyball govern doubles play, with the following exceptions:

- The players need not rotate.
- The ball may be served from *any* area beyond the end line.
- Open-hand "dink" shots are prohibited.
- You may cross the center line as long as you don't interfere with the opposing team's play.

In an effort to ease up a little on the players, games are usually played to 11 points, not 15. Winners must still win by two. Also, a USVBA rule allows the court to be shortened by five feet on each side. This is known as the short court. In a splendid tribute to true macho spirit, *nobody* plays the short court.

With only two people carrying out the chores usually shared by six, strategy in doubles is quite different. Serving takes on an even more important role, with the emphasis on placement rather than power. Both players must stay back to play defense. The pattern of bump-set-spike remains the same, however.

Doubles games are most frequently played on the beach. Sun, shore, sand seem to be natural accompaniments to volleyball. Chapter 8 has been devoted to this facet of the game.

CO-ED VOLLEYBALL

Volleyball is a game that demands quickness, endurance, and skill. Unlike many other sports, it does not depend on power and strength alone. This makes teams of mixed sex very popular. Teams are usually made up of from two to six players, with half the total composition male and the other half female. The only change in rules is the height of the net. It is kept at eight feet (playing height for men). Because the average male is taller than the average female, lowering the net to women's height would actually prove to be of greater advantage to male spikers than to female spikers.

In some areas, other local rule changes may apply. For instance, if the ball is played more than once on your side of the court before being returned, one of the touches must be made by a female. Or, if there are two female players at the net, as there are bound to be sometimes, a male may come from the back court to

A player carefully scouting the opposition and conserving her strength.

block at the net. USVBA allows one back-row male player to come up to the net when there are two women in the front row. All such rules are used to prevent male domination of mixed play.

Another variation of mixed play, *Reverse Co-ed*, lowers the net to women's height but forbids men from leaving their feet when at the net, except to set. This change in the rules, although experimental, has proved popular, especially at tournaments.

THE RULES

The rules governing volleyball play and participants are easy to learn and live by. The following is a short summary of the rules as found in the official rule book of United States Volleyball Association. The complete, unedited, yearly updated rule book may be purchased for a nominal sum from:

United States Volleyball Association
1750 East Boulder Street
Colorado Springs, Colorado 80909

Rules 1, 2, and 3: The Court and Equipment

A volleyball court measures 59 feet (18 meters) long by 29½ (9 meters) wide (*see Figure 2*). Outside the boundary lines, there should be a clear area of 6½ feet (2 meters). The more room to allow for freedom of play, the better. The minimum overhead clearance from floor to ceiling is 23 feet (7 meters). A flat surface is assumed, leaky roofs not withstanding.

FIGURE 2: THE VOLLEYBALL COURT

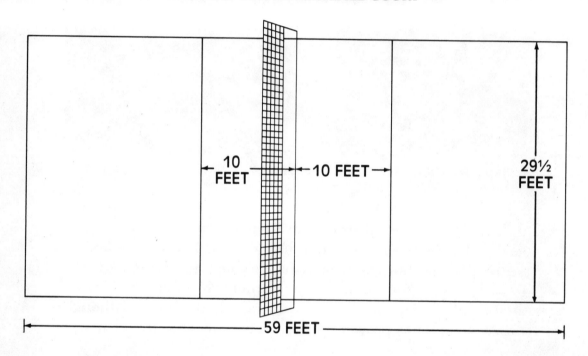

The court is split into two playing halves, divided by the net and a center line running beneath the net. The center line is 2 inches (5 centimenters) wide. The playing height of the net 7'11⅝" (2.43 meters) for men and 7 feet, 4¼ inches for women. The net must be 32 feet long and 39 inches (1 meter) wide. The net must be hung and supported in such a way that it is equidistant from the playing surface at all points between the boundary lines. White tape and antennas should also be affixed to the net at each end immediately above the side lines. For refereeing purposes,

In some playing situations, it is impossible to have the stipulated 23 feet of clear space above the court, due to rings or ropes suspended from the rafters. In a few instances, the roof itself may be less than the required height. Teams should discuss with the referee what is in play *before* play commences. Frequently, so long as the ball does not change sides when it strikes or after it strikes a low obstruction, the ref will allow play to continue. Obviously, it's better to get maintenance personnel to remove the offending apparatus if at all possible.

the antennas are considered part of the net. The net must be kept reasonably tight throughout play.

The ball must be made of 12 or more pieces of the same uniform light color, measure 25–27 inches (62–68 centimeters) in circumference, and weigh at least 9 ounces but not more than 10 ounces.

The court is further divided by an additional line on each side of the net, which runs parallel to the center line and is 10 feet from it. This 10-foot line is the attack line, and it separates back-row players from front-row players.

There are many types of balls on the market today. They may be made of leather or a good-quality imitation leather. Beware of plastic, rubber, or vinyl. They're cheaper than leather or leather-like balls but have a correspondingly shorter life span. They also hurt like hell to hit or pass. Be good to yourself! Buy a good ball. They're worth the investment.

Rule 4: Rights and Duties of Players

Coaches and players are expected to know the rules and play by them. Coaches, managers, and team captains are responsible for the proper conduct of all team personnel. The only player who may address the referee is the floor captain.

Each team is allowed two 30-second time-outs in a game. Only the captain or coach may request a time-out. Such a request must come when the ball is dead. No player may leave the floor during a time-out. A coach may speak to the players during a time-out, but the coach may not enter the playing area.

The following acts are subject to penalty by the game officials:

- addressing the officials concerning their decisions;
- making profane or vulgar remarks;
- shouting, yelling, or clapping hands in an attempt to distract an opponent;
- attempting to influence the decisions of officials.

Any offense committed by coaches, players, or other team members may result in a warning (yellow card) or penalty (red card). Repeated or extremely serious offenses may result in a team member's expulsion from the game or disqualification from the match.

> Poor conduct and circus antics are ruining some sports. In volleyball such behavior is just not permitted. If you can't beat your opponents through your mastery of volleyball skills, have the courage to lose gracefully.

A yellow card is issued for minor offenses such as talking to opponents. A second minor offense results in a penalty. A penalty (red card) is awarded for rude behavior or a second minor offense. If the offending team is serving, they lose the serve. If they are not serving, a point is awarded to their opponents. A second act meriting a penalty results in the expulsion of the guilty party.

Rule 5: The Teams

A team is made up of six players plus substitutes. The total number may not exceed 12 players.

Uniforms should consist of a jersey, shorts, and heelless shoes with rubber or leather soles.

Before the start of a match, each team must submit to the scorer a lineup showing the starting positions of the players.

Usually six substitutions are allowed per team per game;

however, in lower skill levels, 12 substitutions may be allowed, and in recreational volleyball, substitutions may be unlimited. Substitutions can be made at the request of the floor captain when the ball is dead. With six substitutions, a player starting the game may be replaced only once and may subsequently reenter the game only once, and then only in the original serving order in relation to other teammates. Only the original starter may replace a substitute during a game.

Rule 6: Team Areas, Duration of Matches, and Interruption of Play

A coin toss by the team captains determines side and serve for the first game. The winner has first choice. Teams exchange sides after each game. For the deciding game of a match, there is a new coin toss for side and serve. In a deciding game, the teams exchange sides after one team reaches eight points, but the serve remains with the team that was serving.

When the referee perceives a hazard or an injured player on the court, play is stopped. A play-over is called when the game is resumed.

Rule 7: Commencement of Play and Service

After the referee's whistle, the server has five seconds to toss or release the ball for service. When the player contacts the ball, no part of the server's body may touch the end line, the court, or the floor outside the service area. A player serves until a fault is committed by the serving team.

Side-outs occur after these service faults:

- The ball touches or passes under the net.
- The ball touches a member of the serving team before going over the net.
- The ball lands outside the opponent's court.
- The ball fails to pass *entirely* between the two antennas or touches an antenna.

Players rotate one position clockwise after a side-out. All players but the server must be in their proper rotational positions according to the lineup before the ball is served. After the ball is served, the players may take any position they deem appropriate.

The serving team may not screen their opponents from watching the server or the serve.

Rules 8 and 9: Playing the Ball

A team may make up to three successive contacts with the ball before it must be returned to the opponents' court.

The ball may be hit with any part of the body above the waist. The first ball over the net can make multiple contact with a player *as long as* the player makes only one attempt to hit the ball and his or her hands are not in position to set the ball. The ball must not come to rest in a player's arms or hands and must be hit so that it rebounds cleanly. Players may not attack the ball on the opponents' side of the net.

Other than a served ball, a ball that hits the net between the antennas continues to be in play. Should a player touch the net during play, a fault is incurred. There is no such thing as an accidental touch. It is a fault if a player contacts the opponents' area except with his or her foot.

Rule 10: Dead Balls

The ball is dead when any of the following occurs:

- The ball touches the antenna or the net outside the antenna.
- The ball fails to cross the net entirely inside the antennas.
- The ball contacts the floor, a wall, or, any object hanging from or attached to the wall or ceiling.
- A player commits a fault.
- A served ball hits the net or any obstruction.

Rule 11: Team and Player Faults

Teams are penalized for a fault by loss of serve (side-out) or, if not in possession of the serve, by the awarding of a point to the opponents. When players of both teams commit faults simultaneously, a play-over occurs.

The following actions are team or player faults:

- The ball touches the floor or is held or pushed.
- A team hits the ball more than three times in a row.

- The ball touches a player below the waist.
- A player touches the net or antenna or completely crosses the center line.
- A player attacks the ball in the opponent's area.
- A back-row player in the attack zone hits the ball into the opponents' court from a height above the net.
- A ball is played by a player using a teammate as a means of support.
- A player receives a personal penalty.
- A player touches the ball or an opponent by reaching under the net.
- A team receives instructions from any other member on the bench, after having been warned previously.
- A game is persistently delayed or an illegal substitution is made.
- Service is performed out of rotation.

The only time a player may touch the net without penalty is when the ball strikes the net with such force that the momentum causes contact between the net and a player. This is not a foul and should not be called.

Rule 12: Scoring and Results of the Game

The serving team is awarded a point when the receiving team commits a fault. The first team to gain 15 points by a two-point advantage wins the game. A team that cannot field six players to start a game or refuses to start after the referee's request loses the game by default, 15–0.

Rule 13: Decisions and Protests

In most cases, the decisions of the referee and the referee's supporting staff are final. However, in USVBA-sanctioned tournaments, a team may protest a judgment.

Rules 14–17: The Referee and Supporting Staff

The first referee is located at one end of the net during play and has complete authority over the conduct of the match. The first referee may overrule the decisions of other officials.

The second referee stands at the net and opposite the first referee. The second referee assists the first referee by calling such faults as center-line violation and player contacting the net. The second referee also keeps track of time-outs and requests for substitutions.

The scorer is usually located behind the second referee and keeps track of points as they are awarded, the rotational order and serving order of players, the number of substitutions, the number of time-outs, and so on.

The line judges position themselves opposite each other diagonally, in the nonserving corners of the court. Line judges signal whether a ball is in or out of the court area. They also signal a foot fault during service. The first referee may refer to the line judges for assistance in making calls.

In pick-up games, the team that has just lost is frequently responsible for the refereeing chores of the following game. In tournament or league play, individual teams are designated as having responsibility for calling the game. However, if there is no referee, every player is expected and required to call his or her own fouls and to make line judgments during play. Everyone respects a fair player.

1
BUMP

Every sport has a rhythm. Each has its own systematic, harmonious, and consistent method for successfully completing a segment of play. The golfer must assess distance, select a club, and strike the ball. The tennis player has to anticipate the adversary, move to the ball, and strike and place the ball. In volleyball, the players strive for *bump*, *set*, and *hit*.

Because volleyball is a team sport and no player may hit the ball twice in succession, you can learn these segments—bump, set, and spike—one at a time. But only by successfully mastering each phase of the game and learning to blend these skills can you become a well-rounded player.

USING THE BUMP PASS

The bump pass is an essential skill that is often used to initiate the offensive attack. Use it on any ball coming over the net low, fast, and/or with a lot of spin. You can bump whenever you want to pass the ball to teammate in a high, easy trajectory.

At times you may also want to use the bump pass to return the ball over the net. Bumping the ball over the net high and deep gives your teammates the maximum amount to organize a successful play.

One last reason for using the bump pass: it is one of the easiest shots to execute, and the only way you can be called for a foul is if the ball rolls up your arms or comes to rest on your arms.

Hand Position

To use the bump pass, also called the forearm pass, you must join your hands together, in order to avoid any possibility of a double hit. The ball must contact both arms simultaneously. There are several different methods for joining your hands, and they are described as follows.

Options for Hand Position

Wrapped Fist. Loosely clench the fist of your dominant hand and place it in the palm of your opposite hand. Wrap the fingers

Wrapped fist hand position.

of your opposite hand around the outside of your dominant hand. Keep your thumbs side to side, parallel, pointing forward, and resting on top of your index fingers. Keep your elbows locked.

Thumb in Palm. Place either hand in the palm of the other, both palms facing up. Fold the thumb of your lower hand into the palm of the upper. Cross the remaining thumb over the lower. Now force both hands down toward the floor as far as possible. This will cause your elbows to lock and your forearms to rotate outward presenting a broad and flat area of contact.

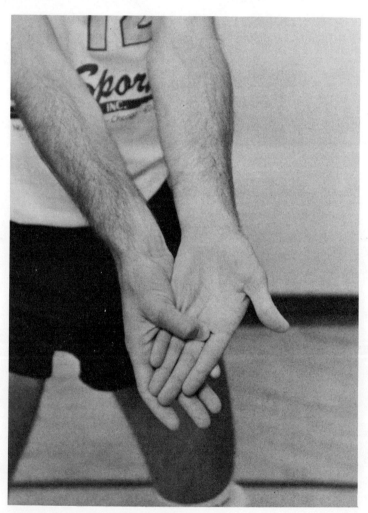

Thumb in palm hand position.

Cupped Palm. The cupped-palm method, while less popular than it once was, is still used by many players. It borrows elements from the wrapped-fist and thumb-in-palm hand positions. Place one hand inside the other as though you were going to make a cup. Now bring your thumbs together side to side, keeping them parallel. Lock your elbows and rotate your forearms outward by forcing your hands down toward the floor as far as possible.

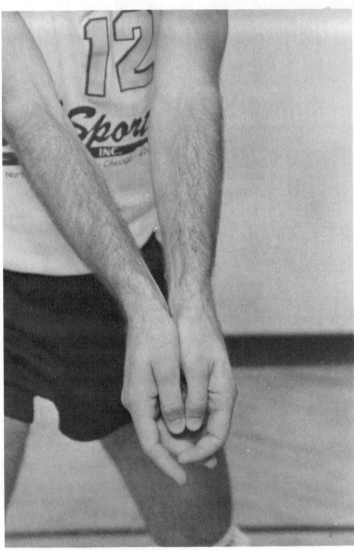

Cupped palm hand position.

Common Characteristics of Hand Positions

These methods have two characteristics in common:

1. *The elbows must be kept locked.* This helps give proper direction to the ball and also presents a broad flat surface for the ball to strike.
2. *The area the ball hits is between the elbow and the wrist.* The forearms are ideally suited to get under a low, hard-driven ball and deflect it upward in an easily controlled arc.
3. *The hands are pressed down toward the floor.* This helps to hyperextend the arms.

Try all three methods and adopt the one that works best for you.

Bumping the ball. This player has shifted his position slightly to play a ball that is a little to his right. Notice how he pushes off with his left foot but his right foot is planted firmly on the floor to provide stability.

TECHNIQUE

Getting in Position

Get ready to make a bump pass by assuming a normal ready position. This means your feet are comfortably apart, a shoulder's width or so. Your knees are slightly bent, with your weight forward on the balls of your feet. Hold your hands loosely at your side.

As the ball approaches, move to it and face your body in the direction you want the ball to go. Once in position, extend your arms fully, using one of the three hand positions just described. *Keep your elbows locked.* Bend your knees so that your arms are parallel to your thighs and your hips are below the path of the ball. Your weight should be on the balls of your feet, and your back should be straight. Your feet should be even or almost even with each other and should still be comfortably apart.

The ready position. The upper arms are kept at the sides, but the lower arms are parallel to this player's thighs.

Contacting the Ball

Hit the ball on the fleshy area of your forearms, above your wrists but below the inside of your elbows. As the ball strikes your arms, shrug your shoulders slightly, keeping your body pointed toward the target, and push up with your legs, straightening your knees. It is this lifting of the legs and shrugging of the shoulders that propels the ball.

Ideally you should hit the ball at waist level. If the ball is higher than waist level, you must either raise your body by straightening your knees or take a step backward. If the ball is too low, bend your knees further or step forward.

Remember not to swing at the ball. The gentle, fluid motion provided by flexing your knees and shrugging your shoulders is all it takes to carry the ball to the target. A hard-hit ball requires no additional momentum. In fact you may have to cushion it in order to control it.

After you have made the pass, return to the ready position and *follow the play*!

Perfect contact in a game situation. This ball was a little high; the player has adjusted by straightening her legs. Even so, her hips remain below the ball.

DRILLS

Practice bumping with a friend by having him or her throw the ball to you in an arc of about six feet and from a distance of six to ten feet. Be sure to return to the ready position after each pass, with your arms loosely in front of you or at your sides and your weight on the balls of your feet. You may want to bounce or shuffle your feet to stay loose and ready to move. It's important to keep your arms relaxed at your sides unless you're actually in position and bumping the ball. You can't move efficiently or

Practicing the forearm pass in a controlled situation.

quickly if you keep your arms outstretched and locked in front of you all the time.

Once you can bump with 80 percent accuracy a ball thrown directly to you, have your partner start moving you around a little: a few feet to the right, a few feet to the left, forward a few steps, backward a few steps. The ball is rarely going to come straight to you on the court, so the sooner you can do this, the better.

It is also possible to practice bumping against a wall.

■ TROUBLE SHOOTING ■

Concentrate on watching the ball and moving it accurately to your target. If you find the ball going too high and well short of your intended mark, check your arm position. Either your arms are bending at the elbows, or they are not parallel with your thighs. If the ball is rebounding off your arms to the right or left, check to make sure your hand position is correct and your arms are even with each other. Remember, you must have a flat, even area of contact. If the ball often goes a few feet wide of the intended target, check the position of your body. More than likely, the vertical midline of your body is not squarely facing the target.

Concentrate on the ball as it comes to you and adjust your body position right up to the moment of contact.

At least initially, bumping is going to give you sore arms. It's only temporary and will ease, then disappear with practice. But use your head. "No gain without pain" is a wonderful saying only if it's someone else's pain. So if you're really sore, cut back on your practice.

2
SET

The set, or overhand pass, is a little more difficult to perfect than is the bump pass. But because the setter can accurately place the ball anywhere in his or her own court, it's the play that sets up every volleyball play.

As the name implies, the set literally sets the ball in position for another player to spike it. If the set is good, just where the hitter wants it, the spike will be powerful—and difficult to return.

Ideally a team must have at least two members who are excellent setters. A good setter is the most valuable player on the team.

HAND POSITION

Choosing the correct hand position for the overhand pass is easy. Unlike the bump, there is only one way to do it. Your hands are three to four inches above your forehead, with your thumbs pointed down toward your eyes and your fingers spread apart loosely and cupped. Your elbows are at roughly a 45-degree angle from the sides of your body. Your wrists are cocked away from

A word on setters. What the catcher is to baseball, what the center is to ice hockey, what the quarterback is to football, the setter is to volleyball. The setter controls the pace and flow of the game with short inside sets or long outside sets. Anyone who uses the overhand pass must have good hands, but a setter must have great hands as well as great feet and a tremendous desire to *get the ball*. Setters must have the anticipatory powers of a fortune teller, the stamina of a long-distance runner, the leadership qualities of a statesman, the patience and mental discipline of a Chinese philosopher. Often, the setter is the best all-around athlete on a team.

Proper hand position for the overhand pass.

Receiving the pass, preparatory to setting.

you. You should be able to see a rough triangle created by the opposing index fingers and thumbs.

This cradle for the ball should be just wide enough to accept the ball. If it's any wider, the ball will go through your hands and, if your position is correct, hit you in the nose. Any closer together, and the ball will bounce off your fingers.

When a ball is successfully spiked, everyone congratulates the hitter. When the ball is hit out of bounds, into the net or into the block, everyone blames the setter. Job, that man of biblical endurance, could have been a great setter.

TECHNIQUE

Move to the ball and turn to face the target (where you want the ball to go). The rules prohibit carrying the ball, so you must move

The finish position after setting. Notice how the player's body is completely extended from toes through fingers.

Another example of good follow-through after a set.

into position quickly. As in the bump pass, keep your knees bent and your back straight, and forward a little. Your feet are about a shoulder's width apart, one slightly ahead of the other for good balance, and your weight should be on the balls of your feet. Bring your hands up into their proper position and look for the ball through the fingers of the triangle you have created above your face.

As the ball drops into your hands and makes contact, wrap as many of your fingers around it as possible, being careful to avoid any contact with the palms. If the ball hits your palms, it is called a push, which is against the rules. Snap the ball out of your hands by accelerating from the balls of your feet, right up to your shoulders, and on through your elbows, wrists, and fingers. Up and out! The ball will seem to flick out of your hands in a high arc to the target area, where a spiker can smash it into your opponent's court.

You must receive the ball *above your forehead* and in line with the rest of your body. Your thumbs and wrists cushion the ball into your hands, on the pads of your fingers, while every joint in your body, including all your fingers, will push it out.

> The proper target area for the setter is the area about two feet inside the sideline and roughly two feet off the net. It is from this general spot that the spikers will end their approach and hit the ball. The setter must constantly visualize this area, never losing track of its distance, much as a sharp-shooting forward in basketball always knows where the basket is.

DRILLS

Initial Practice

To practice the overhand pass, you should cradle the ball in the proper position over your face with your knees bent, wrists cocked, and fingers spread around the ball. Your thumbs should be pointed toward your eyes with your hands three to four inches above your face. Starting from the balls of your feet, up through your whole body, push the ball up and out. Repeat this until the movement becomes easy and natural.

Once you've mastered that, have a friend throw the ball to you in a high arc. First simply try to catch the ball; don't try to set it yet. Just catch it, hold it, then push it out. Gradually increase your speed until the ball never actually comes to rest in your hands at all.

Accuracy

To practice accuracy in setting, toss the ball to yourself, then try to set it into a basketball hoop. The distance from the free-throw line to the basket is about the same as the distance from the setter to the hitting area on a volleyball court. This drill will give you a good feel for the amount of strength required to get the ball into position for the hitter.

Being able to place the ball where you want it is a skill that is developed only over a period of time. The more you practice, the more accurate your sets will be.

▌ TROUBLE SHOOTING ▌

For a beginning setter, the most common error is failure to move quickly to the ball and get under it. Be sure to anticipate the movement of the ball and keep your feet moving.

No play is whistled for a foul more often than the set. Be careful to avoid holding your hands unevenly above your head and juggling the ball as you release it, or you will be called for a double hit. If your hands are too far apart and you allow the ball to come to a complete rest, you will be called for a carry. If you get too much of your hand on the ball, especially if there is a loud slap as you make contact, you will be called for a push. If you drop your hands below your face as you receive the ball, a foul will be whistled as well.

Even though it's difficult, a *legal* set is the most valuable volleyball play because it allows the setter to accurately place the ball where the hitter can spike it into the opponent's court.

Almost everyone is familiar with the regular outside set, or the six, as it is called. But in order to add spice to your offensive life, you will need to at least be aware of the other types of sets that are in use *(see Figure 3)*. Many depend on speed and hitting from the middle of the net.

- *One*—A very quick, low set delivered one to two feet above the net and hit while the ball is still rising. Usually for the middle hitter.
- *Two*—A low set placed two to four feet above the net. Usually for the middle hitter.
- *Three*—A low set usually placed midway between the

Spiking the one set.

Spiking the two set, which is slightly higher than a one set.

setter and the sideline. It should rise no more than four feet above the net—that is 12 feet from the floor. For the middle hitter or the outside hitter.

- *Four*—Also known as a shoot set. A low set placed one foot from the sideline and one to two feet above the net. Usually for the outside hitter.
- *Five*—A high outside *backset*. Usually for an outside hitter.
- *Six*—A regular outside set placed about 10 feet above the net, near the antenna the setter is facing.

Spiking the three set.

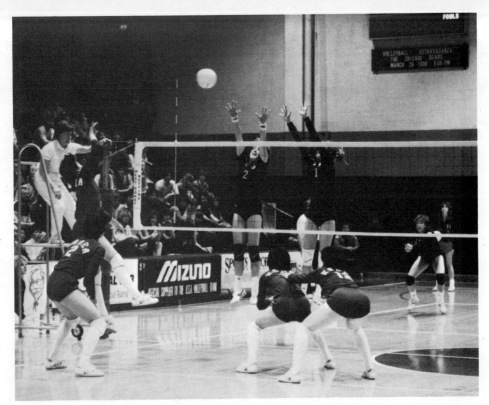

Spiking the four set.

FIGURE 3: PLAY-SET DIAGRAM

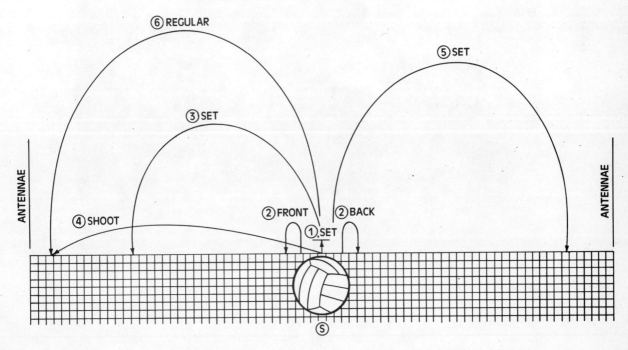

SETTING STRATEGIES

There are several ways for setters to add surprise and diversity to their team's attack. The major setting strategies are the back set and the short set.

Back Set

In the back set, the setter targets the area directly *behind* him or her. If the team you're up against cannot be sure whether the right front or left front hitter is going to be set for a spike, they will be that much slower to set up their defense. Of course the pass to the setter must be on the money. If the pass is so poor that the setter is restricted to setting one hitter, you have lost any chance for surprise.

Spiking the back set.

Until the very last moment, the back set looks precisely the same as a regular set. It is not until you contact the ball that any difference can or *should* be noted. At the moment of contact, take a very short step forward, usually with your left foot. This will help give added push backward. As you begin the upward surge through the ball, your back is arched and your hands and shoulders rotate backward, pushing the ball up, out, and toward the unseen target area. The only physical differences between the regular set and the back set are the short step forward, the arching of your back, and the backward rotation of your hands and shoulders. Otherwise, all actions of your knees, elbows, and wrists are exactly the same.

Double jeopardy. The setter has the option of putting up a one set for the hitter he is facing, or a back two set for the hitter approaching from the rear.

The only reason for using a back set is to catch the opposition unaware. Thus, if a good setter receives a poor pass and won't be able to fool the folks on the other side of the net, he or she will take that extra step, turn, and put up a hittable set. There is no profit in forcing a back set that will surprise no one and that can't be spiked. A safe set and a safe hit keep the game going.

Back setting requires a great deal of practice. Because you have to imagine the target area and have no opportunity to visually assess the distance the ball must travel to the hitter, the back set is seldom as accurate as the regular set. Therefore, although setters must be able to use it. They must not become dependent on it.

Short Set

Just as the back set can keep the other team from keying on just one hitter, so too can short sets in the middle of the court keep the opposition off balance. These quick sets constitute the most exciting plays in volleyball. They require a finely tuned sense of timing, excellent communication between setter and hitter, and pinpoint passing. A good short-set strategy to learn first is the two set.

Two Set. The two set attempts to take advantage of slowness in the opposition and height and quickness in your team, with the emphasis on quickness. It gets its name because it falls into the #2 area in Figure 3.

The play begins with a good pass to the setter. Instead of pushing it out to either side of the net, the setter places it about two to four feet above the net and a few inches away from the setter. If the setter puts up a good two set, the hitter should be able to successfully spike the ball almost every time. The setter must watch for blockers out of the corners of the eyes. If the opposition is forming a two-person block near the center, the setter should go to an outside hitter. The objective is to pass the ball to hitter on one blocker or no block at all. Obviously, the setter must be alert.

Two Set as a Back Set. The two set can also be run as a back set. The setter tries to conceal until the last moment the intended target area, then uses the usual back-set technique, remembering to ease off the backward rotation of hands and shoulders and the upward motion of the rest of the body. The ball should rise no more than four feet above the net and no less than two feet. The ball should be anywhere from six inches to one foot from the setter's back.

Trouble Shooting. In execution, all the setter has to remember is to use a *gentle touch* in pushing the ball up and out. For a good two set, the setter merely needs to get the ball up a few feet. If the ball is set too high, it gives the defense time to form a block. If the ball is pushed too far away from the setter, the hitter will be unable to give it a good hard hit.

Setters must know their hitters and their preferences. For instance, a particularly tall hitter may want a higher set in the middle. If a block forms, who cares? Tall hitters can go over a block. Shorter hitters have to depend on quickness to beat a block. They may want a lower than usual set for a two. Left-handed hitters will have to have the set pushed out more if hitting from the left side of the court. The opposite is true if they are hitting from the right.

Setters must have confidence that hitters are not going to collide with them after they put up a two set. Few occurrences distress setters more than finding that a player's knee is being introduced into their rib cage. Collisions and injuries can be avoided with practice and good communication.

Hitting a Two Set. Some coaches feel it is easier for a novice to hit a two set than a regular outside set. One reason is that many new players generally release too soon, before the ball has been set, but for a two set, the hitter *must* release before the ball has been set.

The hitter must make a straight-ahead approach to the setter. The approach should begin just as the ball arrives in the setter's hands. Hitters should take their usual two- or three-step approach. The ball should be in the air and almost at its peak as the hitter initiates the jump. This set gives the hitter an excellent opportunity to put the ball down. You're hitting from the middle of the court so you have more opportuniteis to hit to a chosen spot, be it long, short, straight down, or dink.

Take your usual power shot and make sure your point of contact with the ball is normal—not too high or the ball will go

The setter has clearly beaten the block on this play and the hitter has a nice, clear shot.

out over the back line or side lines. Not too low: the ball will go into the net on your side. Make use of your peripheral vision and put the ball "where they ain't." Timing and good court sense are more important than raw power.

The two set makes for a very exciting game. It can really open up your team's offense and shake up the opposition. If given enough time in practice, even relatively new players can make good use of it.

3
SPIKE

Every sport has some sort of wonderfully exciting, emotional play that brings the crowd to its feet, cheering wildly. Baseball players swat home runs. Football linebackers stuff runners just as they get to the line of scrimmage. Basketball players slam dunk. And volleyball players hit spikes.

A perfect spike goes something like this:

The ball comes cleanly from the setter's hands, rises high into the air, then begins its fall. The hitter approaches, all the while keeping one eye on the ball, the other on the opposing players. The hitter jumps, winds up, and *wham!* The ball is driven down into an undefended area of the court—or, even better, into an opponent's undefended face. The conquering hero is congratulated by his or her teammates.

The purpose of the spike is either to place the ball where the other team can't return it or to hit the ball so hard that the defenders find it impossible to control.

The most important task is to hit the ball into the playing area. It doesn't really matter how hard the ball is hit if it goes into the net or out of bounds. The effect would be the same if the ball hadn't been hit at all. Until timing and co-ordination are fully achieved, that's the main thing to go for: hit the ball and keep it in bounds.

TECHNIQUE

Approach

The approach is important in the spike because the hitter must jump as high as possible above the net for a good hit. You should be standing eight to twelve feet from the net, depending upon your size. A taller person has a longer stride than a shorter person, so find the distance that's right for you. Many people like to come in on the ball at an angle to the net. That means starting your approach from outside the court. It is not against the rules, so if it suits you, do it.

Starting Position. Your arms should be held loosely at your sides, your weight on the balls of your feet, your knees bent slightly, ready to move forward quickly. Once the setter has placed the ball, the spiker waits until the ball reaches the highest point of its arc. At this instant *and not before*, the hitter starts his or her approach. This phase is crucial to the overall timing of the play. If you start too soon, you arrive before the ball does. If you start too late, the ball arrives before you do.

Three Steps Forward. Usually hitters take three steps in the approach. For a right-handed hitter, the sequence is left foot, right foot, left foot. It is opposite for left-handed hitters. Some people use a two step and hop approach. The last step in the approach is taken by the foot opposite the dominant hand. Thus, if the spiker is right-handed, the last step is taken with the left foot. Some hitters also use a two step and hop approach. With either approach you should finish with the heels of both feet firmly planted on the floor, knees bent, ready for the take off.

Ready to Jump. This closing step enables you to change forward momentum to vertical momentum. Both arms are swung behind you, your weight is on the heels of your feet, you are in a semi-crouched position and ready to jump.

Jump

As you spring upward, your weight will be transferred to the balls of your feet. Simultaneously, your arms swing forward. Your legs and arms drive *straight up* toward the ball as high as possible. At this point, if you started at the correct instant and

Approaching the ball.

Planting the feet, preparing to jump.

took off from the right spot, the ball should be six to twelve inches in front of you and on your right side (if you're right-handed). You should meet the ball *above* the net. As your body is going up, your arm swing continues. When your arms reach face

Jump, point, lock the hitting arm, and . . .

level, the left continues over your head, the right arm is pulled back, bent at the elbow, and cocked, ready to hit. You should almost be able to touch the back of your right hand to the back of your right shoulder.

HIT! This spike will lack full force because the hitter has merely lowered her non-hitting arm, instead of using it to help her follow through.

Your legs should be almost straight out beneath you; their work is done. The upper torso is drawn back from the waist up, away from the ball and the net. You are now ready to explode on the ball.

This series illustrates a nice two-step-and-hop approach, good plant and jump with proper arm swing, and nice form as the hitter is transfixed in mid-air ready to pound the ball.

Hit

As the ball comes into hitting range, your left arm is dropped slightly ahead of the right. It will lead the way as your body rotates forward. The right arm snaps up, out to full extension, and over the ball. Your wrist must be kept loose, because part of the power of the spike comes from the whip-like action of the arm.

You should hit the ball with a completely open or a slightly cupped hand. Don't punch it with your fist. You must place your hand over the top of the ball when both hand and ball are above the net; otherwise the ball will lack top spin and will sail out of bounds.

Landing

What goes up must come down. If your approach was controlled and correct, your re-entry on *terra firma* will be the same. Remember that just as you took off on two feet, so should you land on two feet. Cushion your landing using your feet and knees. Pull your hands and arms away from the net after the hit. Take

care not to spoil a great spike by fouling the net. Be sure to watch your play. As soon as you land, prepare to play defense.

Concentrate on hitting the ball to a specific spot in the opponent's court, instead of just smashing the ball. Concentrating on where you want to place the ball, or even to *whom* you want to hit the ball—for example, to a weak area or to a particular opponent—will help.

DRILLS

Dry Runs

Initial spiking practice should consist of several dry runs. Walk through the approach and jump, concentrating on easy, fluid movements. You must establish a natural rhythm of body movements, so don't leave anything out. Include the heel plant, weight transfer (heel to toe), arm swing, and other movements. Pretend you're moving in slow motion. Point at an imaginary ball with your left arm, hit it with your right, and swing through.

Spiking Without Jumping

Once you feel you have established fluidity in your movements, try spiking a few balls without jumping. Have a friend throw them to you or put them into the air yourself. Make sure you get good top spin on the ball by extending your hitting arm fully at the moment of contact and getting your hand over the top of the ball.

Notice how this hitter has her hitting arm drawn back as far as possible while her left (non-hitting) arm is already leading the way down to give her a good follow-through. The jump isn't too shabby either.

A nice example of full arm extension to get your hand OVER! the ball.

Putting It Together

When you have mastered the first two drills, it's time to start the real thing. Have a friend set the ball by tossing it well above the net, two feet from the side line, and one to two feet back from the net. Integrate all parts of your practice: approach, jump, hit, landing.

Spikers gotta learn to be aware and *sensitive* to changing attitudes in American life. After hitting a novice female player in the stomach with a hard driven ball that left the young lady writhing on the floor, a well known local player stood at the net, silent and anxious, until the injured novice was helped to her feet by her teammates. Seeing that she was re-gaining her breath and her composure, he turned to her boyfriend, who was responsible for dropping this unfortunate lady into some very heavy competition, and called over, "Sorry Tom!" There oughta be a law.

◼◼◼◼ TROUBLE SHOOTING ◼◼◼◼

Spiking is a complicated shot that calls for hand-eye coordination, depth perception, jumping ability, and perfect timing. Nobody said this was going to be easy. Let's go through some of the most common errors hitters make.

MISSING THE BALL. The hitter may sail through the air, completely miss the ball, and land in the net or in the opponent's court under the net. This will happen if the hitter has not properly planted his or her heels in the approach. Forward momentum in the approach must be transferred to vertical motion—height—in the jump. Anything less than a firm heel plant results in a kind of "broad jumping."

LACKING POWER. The hitter may fail to get any power into the spike. Again, the fault is probably in the approach. The hitter is starting his or her approach soon and ends up waiting under the ball or hitting the ball at less than the peak of the jump. Be sure to wait until the ball reaches the top of its arc. Remember, if you're a little late, you can adjust by quickening your approach, but if you're early, you can't go back and start again.

It is also possible that the hitter is contacting the ball too close to his or her body to get some power behind the spike. If the ball lacks power because it is too close to your hitting arm or behind your head, adjust your approach.

GOING OUT OF BOUNDS. The ball may be hit with power but continually go out of bounds. In such a case, the hitter is not making contact over the top of the ball, or else the hitter is snapping his or her wrist insufficiently. This is easy to correct. Make sure you extend your hitting arm fully, and keep your wrist absolutely limp and flexible.

GOING INTO THE NET. The ball may continually go into the net. If a player hits the ball after the peak of his or her jump, on the way down, the ball will not go over the net. The jump must be timed so that spiker and ball meet at the top of the jump.

If you put the ball into the net because you are unable to jump high enough to hit the ball above the net, it does not mean you can't spike the ball. It *does* mean you must receive your set ball further away from the net. Many short players instruct the setter to place the ball five to eight feet back from the net. Instead of trying to hit straight down, they concentrate on hitting "to the line" deep in the opponent's court.

You can increase your vertical jump by using a good weight training program. If you're serious about improving your jump, find a good health club or gym with suitable facilities and talk to the trainer or resident expert. A good long-term program can be established. Dedication and determination can work wonders.

OTHER HITTING TECHNIQUES

Sooner or later, all spikers learn that hitting the ball hard across court just isn't enough to score points. Other players learn where they like to hit, and blockers learn to stuff them. To compensate, a good hitter must learn to be more than a one-trick pony. Besides spiking, hitters must be able to hit down the line, cut around a block, dink, and hit a soft topspin shot.

Line Shot

Hitting the ball across court is a natural tendency for all hitters. It feels comfortable. But to be competitive, a hitter must be able to hit a hard shot down the line.

Technique. To send a ball down the line rather than cross-court, drop your left shoulder and rotate your body in the direction of the hit. The angle of approach and hitting technique are the same as for a cross-court shot. The line shot is especially effective if the right back player of the opposing team has cheated up toward the net and is not expecting a hard-driven ball.

Hitting down the line. The spiker has rotated her body in the direction of the hit. If #8 doesn't move quickly, this play is history.

Trouble Shooting. The most common error in hitting a line shot is hitting the ball out of bounds either to the side line or to the back line. If the ball goes out over the sideline, you've probably exaggerated the rotation of your body. Don't twist around quite so much. If the ball goes out over the back line, you are either making contact too low or failing to get your hand over the top of the ball.

Strategy. Remember to keep in mind that you are not just hitting the ball. You are hitting to a spot on the court, whether it is a

A very well-placed line shot; the hitter shows good body control and court sense. The ball would fall on the line if the woman playing defense wasn't playing her position perfectly.

cross-court power shot or a shot down the line. Although you must concentrate on the ball, you must also use your peripheral vision and depth vision to keep track of what the defense is doing.

Surprise Shots

A hitter who is confronted with a one or two-person block must decide either to hit away and devil take hindmost or to use the block to hide behind and hit a soft topspin shot or a dink. It is

When there's nowhere to go, dink over the block.

impossible to hit away all the time, so a good spiker should know how and when to use these change-of-pace shots.

Soft Topspin Shot. As its name implies, the soft shot is an off-speed hit on the ball. The hitter takes the usual approach and jump but, instead of pounding the ball, hits it just a little late and from beneath instead of over the top. It is hit late in order to drop behind the block. It is hit from beneath to give the ball top spin to make it die as it goes over the net above the outstretched blockers' arms. Most of the action in hitting the ball comes from the shoulder, as the arm rises up toward the ball. A well-executed shot of this type should fall in the middle of your opponent's court, about eight feet behind the block.

Dink or Tip. The dink also uses the block to conceal the intent of the hitter. The spiker simply locks his or her wrist and uses the fingertips of that hand to direct the ball to an area of the court.

Take care not to push the ball on a dink. A dink is considered legal as long as the wrist does not break as the ball is hit.

The dink requires very little effort, just the forward motion of the arm rotating from the shoulder. Deception is the key word.

Number 10 knows there's an acre of open country just behind the blockers, so she goes over them with her non-hitting arm; a very smart technique.

The ball doesn't have to go very far; anywhere just behind or just to the side of the block is enough.

Be sure to face in the direction of the dink. In other words, if you dink to the right of the block you must be facing that direction. [Facing left while dinking right is a definite push or throw.] The dink should be used only against an opponent's block. If there is no block, there is no reason to use an off-speed shot unless your opponents are glaringly out of position.

Confronted with a triple block, this hitter has chosen discretion over valor.

4
SERVE

One of the most important plays in volleyball is the serve. It is the opening attack and can put your opponents at a disadvantage for at least two reasons. First, they can't score while you're serving; only the team that is putting the ball into play can score points. For the opposition to score, they must first win the right to serve. Second, your opponents cannot anticipate where the serve will fall.

The server must stand beyond the end line in a space measuring roughly ten feet from the right sideline toward the middle of the court. The server must not enter the court area or touch any of the boundary lines until after making contact with the ball.

Since every player must serve, each one *must* be capable of putting the ball into play consistently. Volleyball is a rotational

Ideally, there is never any excuse for missing a serve. Every serve that ends in the net or out of bounds is an opportunity lost. It takes momentum away from your team and, even worse, gives possession of the ball to your opponents.

game, and each player must eventually wind up in the right back corner, the server's position. Your first goal is to get the ball into play successfully every time.

Never miss a serve when:
- It is the game point.
- Your opponents have just missed a serve.
- A person you find sexually desirable is watching.
- Your opponents have just rolled off a series of unanswered points.
- The previous server on your team missed a serve.
- Your opponents have just missed their serve at game point.
- You are playing on the beach in front of several hundred people and a local TV camera crew.
- It is the first serve of the game.
- The preceding rally was exceptionally hard fought.

UNDERHAND SERVE

The underhand serve is without a doubt the easiest of all serves to learn. Even though it may not have the same impact as the harder-to-master overhead serve, it's a reliable and consistent method for getting the ball into play.

Hand Position

The ball may be struck with any flat surface of the hand. Many people prefer to use the heel of the hand with the fingers folded back toward the palm. Others like to use the flat surface that is created along the top of the thumb and the index finger when a fist is made. Try to avoid using the knuckles, especially in an uppercut motion. There are too many angles that may cause the ball to veer off. No matter what hand position you decide to use to address the ball, it's important to keep your wrist absolutely rigid when you hit the ball.

Technique

To begin, you should be standing outside the court and in the serving area. Check! You cannot step within the boundaries of the

The spike-serve used by the 1984 Brazilian Men's Olympic team. It requires many, many hours of practice. And they still came in 2nd.

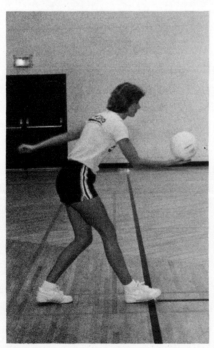

The underhand serve by a left-handed player. Note the foot fault.

court, or a foot foul will be called. Give yourself enough room to take a few steps. You're going to be in motion, not standing still. Ready position is as follows. You should have the ball in your left hand. (Left handers should just reverse these directions written by a right hander for right handers.) Your feet should be comfortably apart, knees slightly bent, facing the direction you are going to serve.

Step forward with your left foot. At the same time, draw your right arm back and bend slightly at the waist. As your left foot touches the ground, shift your weight from back (right foot) to front (left foot). Simultaneously, bring your right arm forward in a pendulum motion and drop the ball or give it a slight throw in front of you. Glue your eyes to the ball! Don't take your eyes off it or pull your head up. Strike the ball with your right hand and follow through with your entire body. When you finish, your weight should be on your right foot, and the ball should be launched into a nice, low arc that easily clears the net and lands in the playing area.

This "simple" serve may sound complicated. It is. That's because all physical movements are complicated when broken into individual segments. Let's go over it again in a slightly different way.

Do your preparation. Out of bounds, in service area, ball in left hand, feet comfortably apart, American Express card not left at home, shoelaces tied, shorts not around knees, etc. Take a walking step forward and hit the ball underhand in mid-step. Got it?

Remember to keep your movements fluid, not jerky. Try to hit the ball as your weight transfers from your back foot to your front. You are using your body weight as well as the strength of your arm to propel the ball. It is not the strength of the arm alone that moves the ball; it is the weight of your body behind your arm at the moment of contact that adds the power. Never depend on your arm alone to serve; the resulting action will throw you off balance and result in inconsistent serves.

Also, keep the drop or toss the same or as consistent as possible all the time. If you release the ball in the same manner every time, it will be in the same place at the moment of contact every time.

OVERHAND SERVE

The overhand serve, or tennis serve, is a little more difficult to master than the underhand. It is the main serve used to today in competition ranging from afternoon pick-up games to the Olympic Games. It is popular because the power that can be put into the serve makes it difficult for opponents to handle. This serve has a very short "hang time." The ball moves so quickly from the server to the defenders that your opponents have little time to field it.

Hand Position

For the overhand serve, the hitting area of the hand is fairly specific. You should use an open or slightly cupped palm. Either position exposes plenty of flat contact area to the ball. Whichever you use, be sure to keep your wrist and hand rigid. This will impart the greatest amount of force to the ball.

Technique

First, check your position. Develop this habit now, and you'll never embarrass yourself in a game situation. Your feet should be comfortably apart, the ball should be in your left hand (if you're right-handed) and you should be far enough away from the end line so that no foot foul is possible.

Toss the ball overhead about three feet or so and slightly to your left. As the ball reaches the top of its arc, take a walking step forward, leading as you normally would with your left foot and pushing off with your right. Raise your right arm and bend it back at the elbow, drawing your upturned hand back toward you shoulder and almost touching it. As your weight transfers from your right foot to your left, reach up and out as the ball drops into range, extending your arm and hitting the ball. Follow through, bringing your arm smoothly down to your side.

You should finish with your arm almost straight out at

Hitting an overhand serve. The player selects an area or target; begins her toss; maintains concentration and initiates arm swing; continues arm swing and begins to move forward; prepares to hit as the ball comes into range; and follows through.

shoulder level or a little lower. Most of your weight should be on your left foot, and the toe of your right foot should rest on the floor, preparing you to step into the playing area.

> Always take a deep breath before you serve, then let it out as you hit the ball. It helps you concentrate.

DRILLS

The best way to practice the underhand and overhand serves is to go out with a friend an hour or so before you plan to play. Find an empty court or pace off an imaginary one, and practice serving to each other.

Once you are able to put the ball into the receiving area on a regular basis, then try to place the ball exactly where you want it—when the real fun begins.

STRATEGY

There are two things to consider when aiming your serve: who you want to receive it and where you want it to go.

Picking a Receiver

If you know a person on your opponent's team is a poor or inconsistent passer, serve it to that person. Some servers like to make eye contact with the person they intend to serve to; intimidation can be a useful tool. If your opponents attempt to adjust to cover up for a weaker player, serve to the position they have left open. Even if they are fortunate enough to get the ball up and avoid the ace, they will be out of position and confused.

One of the most difficult positions to play in serve reception is middle back. Because this back-row player must pinch up to cover the center of the court, a serve that comes to the middle back player at head or shoulder height is difficult to receive. If he or she hesitates, it will confuse the right and left backs, whose responsibility it is to cover him or her. Often this situation leads to the middle back ducking at the last second and an ace for the server.

Picking a Target Area

In general, the best areas to serve to are those that the other team has the most trouble covering. Figure 4 illustrates these areas.

FIGURE 4: TARGET AREAS FOR SERVING (OPPONENT'S COURT)

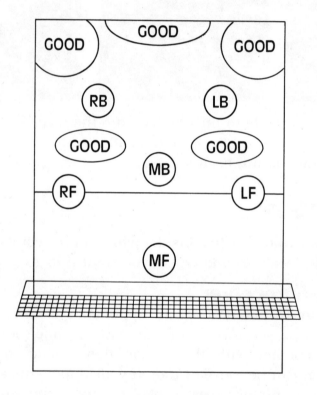

Notice that all the areas marked Good are either between players, so that someone has to call the ball in order to take it, or else so far from the net that a back-row player must pass the ball. Many times, especially with an inexperienced team, calling for the ball is all that is necessary to force a bad pass or a breakdown in comunication that will result in a point for your team.

> Never serve the ball just to get it in play. Always have a particular person or area in mind. Consciously try to force the opposition to make a mistake.

ADVANCED SERVES

In the serve, there are many ways to hit the ball. Each method will impart to it unique movement. Some will cause the ball to dance back and forth in the air; some will cause it to suddenly drop in flight; others result in it suddenly curving toward an unprepared player. Because of the individual nature of serving and the uniqueness of each player, mastery of these trick shots requires a great deal of practice and experimentation.

Float Serve

The underhand serve, simple as it is, can be turned into a more potent weapon by giving it "float" qualities. A floating serve has little or no spin on it. It is so still that the manufacturer's label is not only clearly visible as the ball travels through the air, it is also clearly readable. Because of this lack of movement, the ball tends to move erratically as it attempts to find its own center of gravity.

Underhand Floater. To serve a floater first locate the air valve on the ball. You want to hit the ball either on the air valve or directly opposite it. Once you have selected the proper area of the ball to hit, go through your normal serving procedure, but *do not follow through* after you hit the ball. Stop dead. This type of serve needs to be jabbed, not whacked, so keep minimal contact between ball and hand. The result should be a low serve with a fairly long trajectory in which the ball seems to be wobbling through the air. Even if you serve overhand, this is an excellent serve, even if only for a change of pace. If you only serve underhand, this serve is a necessity. Instead of just getting the ball into play, you may force an error on the receiving team.

Overhand Floater. The overhand floater is similar in technique to the underhand floater. The desired point of contact is the valve or the area of the ball immediately opposite the valve. The preparation and execution are exactly the same as for a regular overhead serve, up to the moment of impact. When you strike the ball, completely stop moving your arm and hand. There is no follow through. Because the point of contact is over your head, not below your waist, the overhand floater has a somewhat flatter trajectory than the underhand, but the effect is the same. The ball seems to dance or wobble through the air with little or no spin.

Technique. There are basically two hand positions for this serve: a semi-fist made by bending the fingers toward the heel of the hand or an open hand, either flat or somewhat cupped. No matter which you prefer, you must keep your wrist rigid and keep contact with the ball to a minimum.

Because making the ball's flight as erratic as possible requires striking a specific area of the ball, you may want to give it a shorter than normal toss before serving. This will make it easier for you to hit the ball accurately. If you toss the ball too high, it may rotate so that you can't hit it on the target area.

Topspin Serve

Although it has fallen out of favor in some circles, the topspin serve, sometimes called the *Brazilian jump serve*, after the team that used it first in international competition, can be a formidable weapon. As with the ordinary tennis serve and the overhand floater, you initiate the serve by tossing the ball overhead, this time relatively high, about three or four feet. You make contact on the lower half of the ball. Your hand is open, with fingers slightly spread and wrapped around the ball at the time of contact. The wrist breaks over the top of the ball, imparting a strong spin. The arm and body follow through completely. For this serve you need a maximum of contact and wrist action.

If you do this serve properly, the ball crosses the net and then suddenly and unpredictably takes a dive. It drops straight to the floor. This is caused by the snapping of the wrist and the action of the hand.

The topspin serve is harder to master than the floating serve. And because it is unpredictable, at least initially, it is not considered a "safe" serve. Should you fail to get enough topspin on the ball, or if you hit the ball too hard, it will go out of bounds. Should you throw the ball too far to your right or left, it will go out of bounds. That's what practice is for. Aim for the middle of the receiving area at first and don't try to overpower the ball. As you gain accuracy and confidence, try to move the ball around the court. If you force an error in the middle of the receiving team's court, there are five other players who may be able to correct the situation. If you force an error on the backline or the sidelines, you reduce the recovery odds considerably.

Curve Ball Serve

The technique for using the topspin serve can also be used to force the ball to curve. The curve ball serve is primarily used on the beach. You can achieve the curving effect by addressing the ball as though it were a topspin serve until the moment of impact. Instead of hitting over the top of the ball, contact it off center, on either the right side or the left. This will cause the ball to curve suddenly to one side or the other. A ball struck on the right side will curve to the right. The opposite is true of a ball struck on the left.

A well executed curve ball creates a great many coverage problems for the receiving team. A player who calls the ball, taking a position based on the imagined line of flight of the ball, sees it veer away beyond reach and perhaps toward a player unprepared to play it.

This serve requires a great deal of practice for most people, although some are able to master it almost naturally. Like the topspin serve, the curve ball serve is not considered "safe." If you try to place it too close to the sidelines, it may go out of bounds when it breaks. That is why, unlike the topspin serve, this serve should be aimed at the middle of the reception area. Experiment with it. You only have to do it well once in a game to cause apprehension in your opponents for a considerable time thereafter.

All players need at least two of these serves in their repertoire. If you have the time to practice and master more than two, you are that much better off. You will know you've reached the peak of your form when you see the knees of your opponents shake as you prepare to serve.

5
DIGGING AND BLOCKING

Now that you've learned to serve, bump, set, and spike, it's time to learn the basics of how to defend against them. Two fundamental defensive techniques are digging and blocking.

DIGGING

If spikers are the glory guys of volleyball, diggers are the forgotten folks in the trenches. Players usually receive more adulation and recognition for how they play at the net than for how they play in the back court. In spite of this, a good defensive dig creates offensive possibilities for your team and delivers a psychological blow to your opponents. Outside of being stuffed on a block, nothing irritates the fragile ego of hitters like a good dig.

Technique

The proper stance and execution for a dig are approximately the same as for a bump, with the following exceptions. Your weight should be further forward, almost on your toes; your

The digger takes a position; but notice how he adjusts his position right up to the moment of contact with the ball. His arms maintain the proper angle as he shifts forward to make the pass and keep his balance.

knees are bent more deeply and may actually extend over your toes; your hips must be kept very low in order to get under the ball. Contact the ball with both arms parallel to the floor and the smallest possible angle between your arms and the ball. The smaller this angle, the greater your chances of keeping the ball on your side of the net.

At the moment of impact, your arms remain motionless, then they spring or bounce back while your body moves forward slightly in a thrusting motion. This helps absorb some of the impact from the ball. Many beginning players are tempted to jump at the ball or swing their arms at it. This results in loss of control. You must contact the ball smoothly, so that it will rebound in a high, controlled trajectory and a teammate may set it.

Drills

No one willingly places themselves in the path of a speeding object. A hard-spiked ball can travel at speeds of over 60 mph. To be good diggers players must overcome their natural fear of being hit and/or hurt by a hard-hit ball. This is best done under a controlled situation supervised by a skilled player. Each novice in turn takes a digging position, while the spiker hits a soft shot

to each from eight to ten feet away. As the new diggers gain confidence and poise, the hitter can increase the velocity of the ball. To imitate a game situation, the hitter can stand on a table or chair placed at the net and hit to players guarding the line or power alley.

Strategy

It is important for diggers to be able to read the opponent's set. If the set is close to the net, defensive players must move up in anticipation of a sharp-angle hit. If it is off the net, defensive players should move back in anticipation of a long shot. The spiker's approach can also give diggers a clue as to where the spiker intends to place the ball. We will discuss proper back-line coverage in Chapter 7, "Defensive Strategy."

BLOCKING

The purpose of the block is to take the starch out of a spike just as it is beginning. It prevents your opponents from using their primary weapon, the spike. It can also be used to take away a hitter's favorite shot, be it cross-court or line, and force him or her to hit into your defense, where the ball can be safely returned.

Technique

The blocker's starting position is as close to the net as possible. There is no need to take approach steps preparatory to a block. Approach steps should be used only by players who cannot get above the net any other way. *Beware!* Broad jumping into a block results in loss of control during the descent. You may commit a foot fault, touch the net, or collide with another player.

A triple block by the United States Women's team turns back another attack.

Proper technique in blocking. The blocker times his jump so that he reaches the highest point of his jump after the ball is hit.

Keep your hands open and at about shoulder level. Concentrate on the hitter across from you. After the ball is set, move into position opposite the descending path of the ball but keying on the hitter's approach. Move by using a side step or crossover step; do not turn and run.

Take a position either directly opposite the ball's path or about one foot inside the path. Taking the position directly opposite the set (facing the path of the ball) guards against a line shot; setting up inside the ball's path guards the cross-court angle.

Begin to jump just an instant *after* the hitter jumps. Remember to key on the hitter, not the ball. The jump should come from as deep a squat as possible in order to take full advantage of your calves and thighs and gluteus muscles. Move your hands down toward your hips and then, as you uncoil, drive them straight up over your head and over the top of the net. Keep your hands apart, your fingers spread and rigid. At the top of your block, your thumbs should be about three inches apart, so the ball cannot be hit between your hands. As your hands rise above the net, break your wrists toward the ball and extend your arms over the plane of the net. This will keep the ball from "dribbling" to your side of

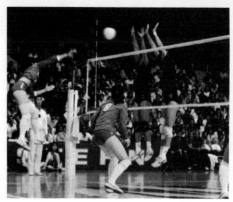

Nice coverage and excellent timing will prevent this ball from crossing the net.

the net after it makes contact with your hands. The descent from the block is the same as the spike. If you went up in a controlled fashion, you should come down the same way.

Shorter players should use the technique of soft blocking. Instead of attemping to penetrate the plane of the net, the blocker's arms and hands remain parallel to the net or are tilted slightly backward. The hands and wrists should remain somewhat loose to absorb some of the ball's impact. A ball coming off a soft block should remain on the blocker's side of the net, where either the blocker or a teammate can play the ball up. The soft block can also be used when the ball is set away from the net.

Double Block

The double block uses two players to cover as much of the spiker's hitting area as possible. In this play, the middle front player moves laterally to close the distance with the end blocker, either the right or left front player. The end blocker establishes the position for the block. Unless they differ in height or jumping ability, both blockers should leave the floor simultaneously, positioning their hands so that the ball cannot be hit between them. This is known as "closing the block." The spiker must not be allowed to hit between the two blockers. If properly executed, the tandem block takes away the hitter's line shot and the cross-court shot. This leaves the hitter only the options of a hard cut shot along the net, a soft shot, or a dink.

The two players in this series show good timing and team play as they jump together, close the block, surround the ball and maintain concentration, and follow the ball after the block.

◼ TROUBLE SHOOTING ◼

Blocking is one of the most difficult volleyball fundamentals. It takes precise timing, ability to read a hitter, alertness, and quick feet. Here are some common errors and a remedy for each.

MISSING THE SPIKE. If you consistently miss the spike, don't jump with the hitter; jump an instant afterwards. Also, keep your eyes on the ball after it is hit. Blockers must see every ball that goes past them. Believe it or not, some people close their eyes as the spiker hits the ball.

The blocker failed to extend over the net and the ball is coming down on her own side.

BALL BETWEEN BLOCKERS. In a tandem block, if the ball goes between blockers, the middle blocker is not closing the block. This may be due to slowness or a lack of anticipation.

The blocker in this photo set up too far from the net and the spiker has taken full advantage of the error.

Middle blockers must keep their feet in motion and resist the temptation to stand flat-footed while watching the setter.

TOUCHING THE NET. If blockers touch the net, this may be caused by extending too far over the net, bending at the waist, or uncontrolled jumping. Blockers must learn how far they can safely penetrate the net. Avoid any bending at the waist. Uncontrolled or wild jumping may indicate poor jumping technique, but it usually indicates the blocker was out of position to begin with.

REBOUNDING BALL. If the ball rebounds from the block in front of the net on the blocker's side, the block is too far away from the net. Get closer. This does not apply to the soft block.

All blockers get caught out of position once in a while. If you're out of position, you still have three options at your disposal:

1. *The one-arm block.* Get into the air and get at least one hand up and in the general area of the ball. Maybe you'll get lucky.
2. *The rainbow block.* Jump and sweep both arms across the net in an arc. Perhaps the gods will smile on you.
3. *The lookout block.* Turn to the back-row players and scream as loud as you can, "Look out!" Should any of them survive the spiker's attack, pick them up and dust them off. Say you're sorry.

Number 12 was out of position to block and she knows it. She's executing a rainbow block in an attempt to close with #14.

6
OFFENSIVE STRATEGY: PUTTING THE BALL DOWN

Now that you know how to hit the ball, you have to learn how to get together with five other people to form a winning strategy. The purpose of the offense is to score points. This can be accomplished only when the team operates with precision and confidence. Team members must understand their individual duty to maintain training, hone their skills, and develop a style of play that is in keeping with the team's ability.

KNOW YOUR TEAM

The team's tactics must be based on the individual players' skills, ability, and understanding of the game. The higher the overall level of the players, the greater the complexity of the offense. A team that passes accurately and has good setters can dazzle and befuddle the defense with a variety of offensive options.

It is courting disaster, however, to impose a sophisticated system of offense on a team that has not completely mastered volleyball fundamentals. Some offenses are flashier than others;

new plays are more in vogue than some older ones. But if an offense or a type of play is too complicated for your team, don't use it. The style of offense must mesh with the caliber of the team. Keep your play selection compatible with your team's skills.

OFFENSE ABCs

Offensive strategy can be sophisticated, but its foundation rests on a few basic principles.

- The classic and most basic passing pattern in volleyball—bump, set, spike—is aimed at providing opportunities to spike the ball for a point.
- The spike is the number-one offensive weapon. The best pass pattern is designed to get the ball into perfect spiking position.
- When a ball is played, whether on a serve or volley return, the first move should be to pass the ball to the setter (positioned in the middle front of the court near the net). The setter sets the ball to either the left or right front player. The spiker then slams the ball into the opponents' court. The pass-set-spike play is the foundation for building all other offensive strategies.

Discussion of strategy requires naming the positions of the players. Figure 5 shows a standard way of referring to these positions by number and the corresponding names of the positions. The numbers also correspond to the order in which the players serve.

SERVE RECEPTION

Seen from above the court, the formation for basic serve reception looks like an M *(see Figure 6)*. The setter (middle front) does not take part in serve reception. The second ball goes to the setter, only to the setter, and to no one else. The only exception to this is when the initial pass is so errant that the setter cannot get to the ball. In such an instance, the setter must communicate to the team that *help!* is required.

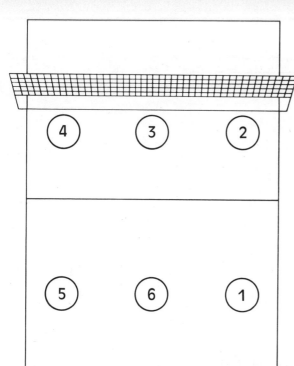

FIGURE 5: NUMBERING POSITIONS
1. *Right Back (RB).*
2. *Right Front (RF).*
3. *Middle Front/Setter (MF/S).*
4. *Left Front (LF).*
5. *Left Back (LB).*
6. *Middle Back (MB).*

A co-ed team set up to receive the serve. The setter faces her own team, waiting for the pass.

FIGURE 6: THE M-FORMATION IN SERVE RECEPTION

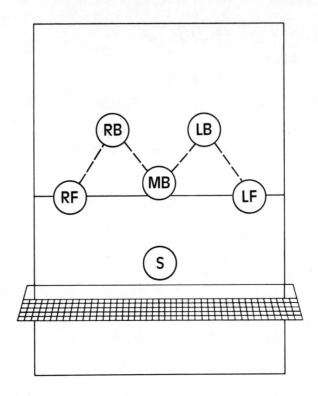

Playing the Serve

The majority of serves fall into the middle area of the court. The players in the RB, LB, and MB positions have primary responsibility for serves to the middle area or longer serves to the corner. It is necessary for whoever intends to play the serve to call his or her intentions as early as possible. This helps all members of the team. The setter knows from what area the ball will be played up. The hitters can begin to adjust their positions in anticipation of a spike. Other floor players can begin thinking in terms of covering the serve receiver.

Players should *never* take their eyes completely off the ball after a teammate has called it. Should an error occur, everyone must be ready to play the ball or make a save. When the ball is called, the entire team should turn toward the caller. This is known as opening up or opening out.

It is especially important for the players in the RB and LB positions to back up the players in front of them in the LF, MB, and RF positions. Should one of the front players call for and then be unable to play the serve, one of the two corner backs must be in a position to take the ball. The player in the LB position backs up the player in the LF position; RB backs up RF. Both of the corner backs cover for the MB position.

Role of the Setter

The setter waits for the serve with his or her back to the net. In this way the setter can observe the direction of the serve and turn or even take a short step toward that area. Setters must be vocal and encouraging, but calm. It is up to them to control the rhythm of the game, keep their hitters "hot," and set all areas of the court accurately. They must avoid negative feedback and caustic comments. If the setter becomes confused, so does the rest of the team. If the setter is calm and confident, so is the rest of the team.

An upbeat attitude can mold a team into a highly motivated, self-confident, winning machine.

The setter can call plays by displaying a given number of fingers as a prearranged signal to the hitters. Or the setter may use coded words to designate who is getting what kind of set. For instance, "blue" may indicate a regular outside set for the LF hitter and a back two for the RF hitter. "Cadillac" may call for the RF hitter to loop all the way over to the left side for a three set, and the LF should be ready for a four or shoot set.

After the ball is played up, it becomes the responsibility of the setter. And the fun begins.

THREE-THREE OFFENSE

The three-three offense is one of the earliest types of strategies used in volleyball. It pairs each hitter with a setter *(see Figure 7)*. A setter gives the ball only to the hitter he or she is paired with.

This strategy has fallen out of favor because it limits setting possibilities. No matter how you do it, if the setters cannot double as hitters, a team finds itself with two setters in the front row every other rotation.

FIGURE 7: STARTING LINEUP OF HITTERS AND SETTERS IN
THE THREE-THREE OFFENSE

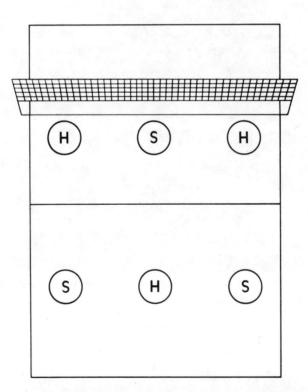

Blockers find it easy to key on the lone hitter. After one rotation the MF hitter in Figure 7 will face a triple block for every set. Nowadays, this offense is used only on beginning teams that are long on setters and short on dependable hitters.

Some life can be infused into this system by switching when there is only one hitter in the front row. The hitter goes to the LF position, and the setter to the usual MF position. If the setter mixes outside sets with quick inside sets, it is possible to deceive and beat the other team's blockers.

FOUR-TWO OFFENSE

As players gain experience, they begin to specialize. The four-two offense takes advantage of this in a way that is best suited to players who are competent but not expert. It employs four hitters and two setters *(see Figure 8)*.

The most common way to start the game is with the setters in the middle of the front and back rows. Hitters are also started opposite each other. The best hitter starts in the LF position, the

FIGURE 8: STARTING LINEUP OF HITTERS AND SETTERS IN THE FOUR-TWO OFFENSE

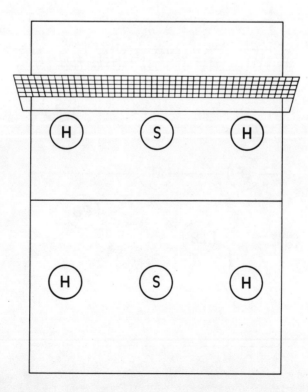

second best in the RB. The weakest hitters occupy the LB and RF positions. The better of the two setters is usually on the same line as the best hitter.

Options After Rotation

Once the team has rotated and the setter has moved to the RF position, you may use several options. The team in Figure 9 is in service reception with the setter in the RF position. The team will pass right to the setter. The setter may set the middle player (MF) or the outside hitter (LF). The advantage of this option is that there is a minimum of movement along the net. Also, if the MF player is a particularly good blocker, it keeps this player available to block the middle, the left, and the right.

The team also has the option of passing to the middle. After the serve, the setter moves quickly to the usual central area near the net *(see Figure 10)*. This adds the possibility of a quick set in the middle. Additionally, keeping the setter in the middle takes advantage of the average player's natural tendency to pass to the middle.

FIGURE 9: PASSING RIGHT WITH THE SETTER IN THE RF POSITION

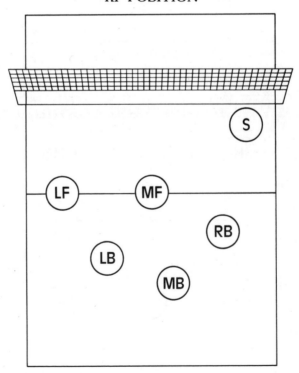

*FIGURE 10: SWITCHING THE SETTER TO THE MIDDLE
FROM THE RF*
Notice that the RB must be careful not to
overlap the front-row players.

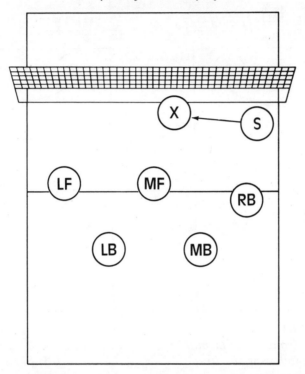

Other methods of switching may be used to keep the strongest hitter in the LF position for as long as possible *(see Figure 11)*. (All techniques for switching are shown for the serving team.) Remember, a right-handed hitter will not hit better from the left side of the court because the ball does not cross the midline of the hitter's body. The opposite is true for left-handed hitters.

If your team is receiving the serve, you may find it impossible to switch the hitters around until after the ball has been passed or there is a slight break in the action. The most difficult switch is bringing a hitter from the RF position to the LF position. The further a player has to go and the more players involved in switching, the greater the likelihood that something will go wrong (Murphy's Law). For this reason, your team must practice switching over and over under scrimmage situations so that every player knows where to go, when to go, and *how* to go. Running into each other at the net falls under the category of giving solace and comfort to the enemy. People are going to laugh at you.

FIGURE 11: SWITCHING THE STRONGEST HITTER

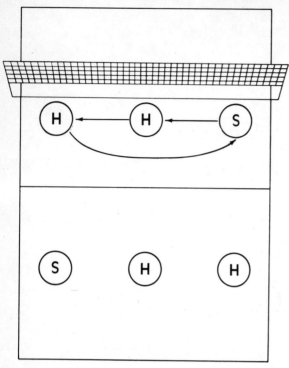

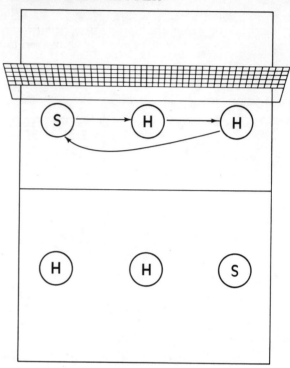

FIGURE 11A

Switching the strong hitter from MF to LF and the setter from RF to MF following the first rotation in the four-two.

FIGURE 11B

Switching the strong hitter from RF to LF and the setter from LF to MF following the second rotation in the four-two.

Using Deception with the Four-Two

Deception can easily be used in the four-two offense to fool blockers. With the setter in the middle position, one or both of the hitters can circle around the setter and confuse the blockers. In Figure 12, the RF hitter goes into motion and approaches the net on the left half of the court. Unless the blocker opposite the RF hitter follows along the net, there should be only one blocker or no blockers at all for the middle hit. If a block does form, the setter can still send the ball to the outside LF hitter, who should have no more than one blocker to beat.

The RF hitter can also be used as a decoy. Figure 13 shows the path of the RF hitter using an approach just inside the path of the LF hitter. The RF hitter fakes the hit and allows the ball to pass by.

FIGURE 12: THE PLAYER IN MOTION

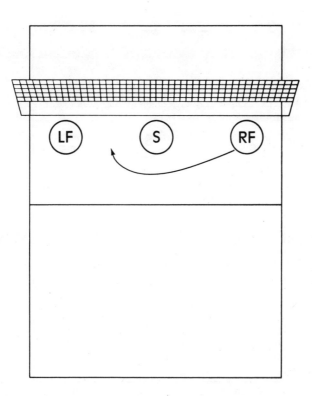

The LF then hammers it home. Unless the blockers are alert, they will go for the decoy and leave the real spiker with an open shot.

One further variation should be added here for hitters. Strictly speaking, it has no special relevance to the four-two offensive system; it can be used in any strategy. Most hitters like to be set within one foot or so of the net. It is easier to keep track of what the blockers are up to and, quite simply, most spikers have more success nearer the net. For those hitters who are able, however, it is a nice variation to use an occasional deep set, about four to six feet back from the net. Because of the extra distance between the point of contact and the net, a spiked ball coming from a deep set disturbs the timing of the blockers—not a lot, but just enough so that if they jump when the spiker jumps (as they're supposed to), the block is totally ineffective. This play can have especially good results when used with the player in motion as a decoy. The decoy takes an approach close to the net and fakes the hit;

FIGURE 13: THE PLAYER IN MOTION AS DECOY

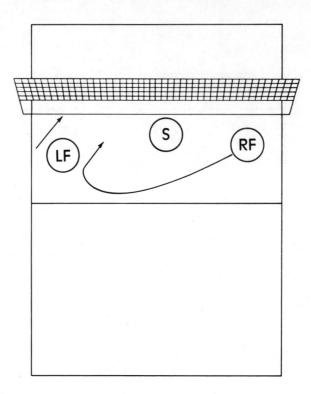

the real spiker hits the deep set from behind.

Using a variety of sets, hitting from the middle, and running decoys can be extremely effective for a team that is willing to practice often enough and long enough to achieve the smoothness that these offensive techniques demand. For many teams, however, there is simply too little time to allow for extensive team practices. So long as hitters and setters understand the basics of switching and the importance of getting the setter to the middle, even a pick-up team can effectively run the four-two. A setter who can accurately back set should still be able to freeze blockers and get the ball to the hitter who can get the job done.

SIX-TWO OFFENSE

The Rolls-Royce of offenses is the six-two. The setters in this offensive system must double as hitters when they get to the net.

Hence, all six starters will be used as hitters, and two of the starters will double as setters.

Number 8 released from the right back position at the instant the ball was served. She will set from the middle front position, then return to right back to play defense.

FIGURE 14: STARTING ORDER FOR THE SIX-TWO OFFENSE
Note positions of setter-hitters.

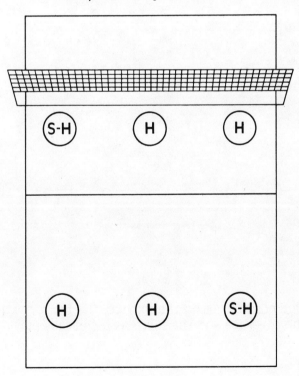

Switching with the Six-Two

The six-two makes maximum use of firepower. All front-row players are hitters *(see Figure 14)*. The setter must come from the back row to set. The setter's position at the net remains the same: just to the right of the middle of the court between the MF and RF hitters. The three diagrams in Figure 15 show the path of the setter from the three back court positions to the proper setting area at the net.

Serve reception positions using the six-two. The front-row players are all involved in the coverage and the setter is technically playing right back.

FIGURE 15: POSSIBLE PATHS FOR SETTER

FIGURE 15A
Path of setter coming from RB position.

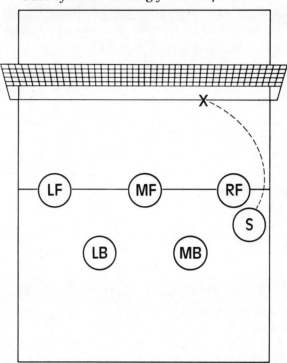

FIGURE 15B
Path of setter coming from MB position.

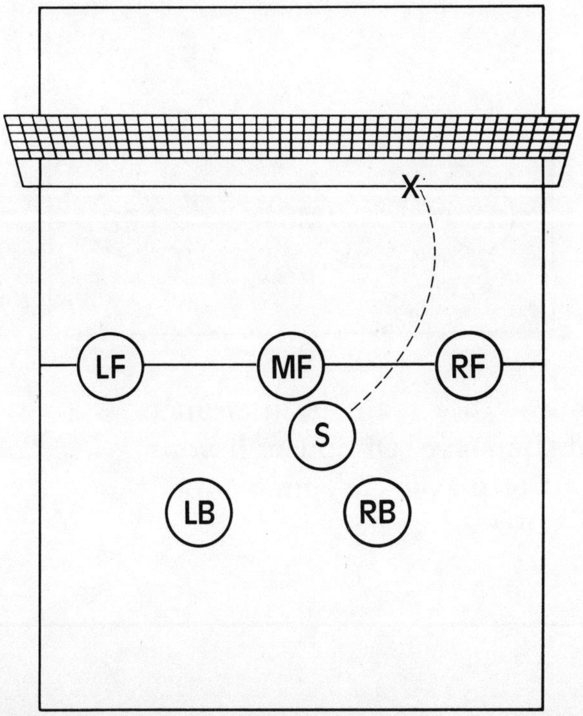

FIGURE 15C
Path of setter coming from LB position.

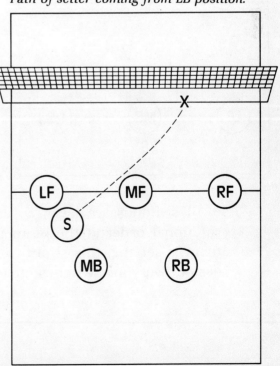

Once the setter has set the ball and covered the hitter for a possible blocked spike, he or she goes to the back court to play defense. On defense the setter plays the RB position *only*, no matter where this player was playing in the rotation prior to the serve. When the setter is in the RB position to begin with, this is no problem. If the setter is in either of the two other back-court positions, the other players must switch to vacate the RB position *(see Figure 16).*

FIGURE 16: VACATING THE RB POSITION

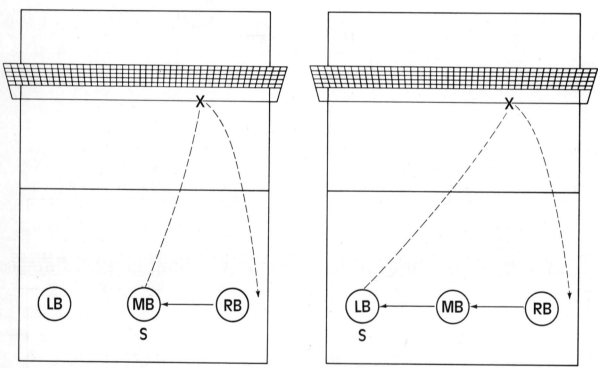

FIGURE 16A
RB switching to MB and setter coming from MB to net, then to vacated RB position.

FIGURE 16B
RB switching to MB, MB switching to LB, and setter coming from LB to net, then to vacated RB position.

All switches are legal, so as long as the team is in proper rotational order at the moment of the serve. Of couse, if your team is serving, this shunting about of players becomes much easier. Everyone switches after the serve.

The setter comes from the RB position for two reasons:

1. The line from the RB position to the setting area is the shortest and most direct. The less distance the setter has to cover, the more attention the setter can give to the set and to what the other team is up to.

2. Of all positions on the floor, the RB has the least chance in being involved in the first defensive play. Once the setter-RB sees another player dig the ball or a free ball is called, the setter releases from the defensive position and goes to the net to set.

> Setters in the six-two offense are the *crème de la crème*. They must be fast, extremely alert, intense, and tireless. They must read defenses and call the right plays. Their hands must be good, to set properly, but their feet must be even better, to get them into position on offense and defense. They must have tremendous desire to get to the ball. Good anticipation doesn't hurt any either.

Advantages of the Six-Two

Having three hitters at the net gives a team the absolute maximum in terms of offensive options. With two outside hitters and one middle hitter, the blockers will find it difficult to put more than one blocker on one hitter. That brings the confrontation down to a one-on-one situation. Occasionally, it is possible to fool blockers completely and leave the hitter with a completely unobstructed shot. Figure 17 shows the different angles each hitter has in spiking from the middle and hitting regular outside sets. If your team uses only the regular outside set, the three set, and the two set, the setter has the option of selecting any one of nine combinations (three hitters times three sets). Not only do the defenders have to worry about *where* the ball is going to be set, they also have to consider *what kind* of a set will be used. These options grow when you add back sets, the player in motion, and decoy hitters.

FIGURE 17: FIELDS OF FIRE: SPIKING ANGLES IN THE SIX-TWO OFFENSE

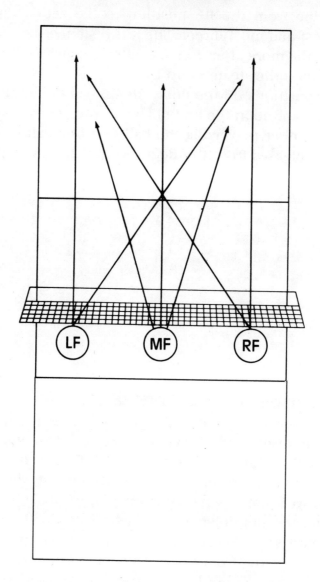

The six-two has been used by Olympic teams in the past. It's simply one of the best offensive systems anyone has yet thought of. But it's not for everyone. It can be used successfully only by teams that have the necessary talent in passing and serious commitment to practicing. It is far better to run a smooth and efficient four-two than a stumbling and mediocre six-two.

FIVE-ONE OFFENSE

As one might suspect, the five-one offense is a cross between the four-two and the six-two offenses. This offense is the one most of the Olympic teams are using today. It is used in precisely the same way as the six-two, with the setter starting in the RB position and continuing to come from that position as the team rotates *(see Figure 18)*. However, when the setter rotates to the

FIGURE 18: STARTING ORDER FOR THE FIVE-ONE OFFENSE

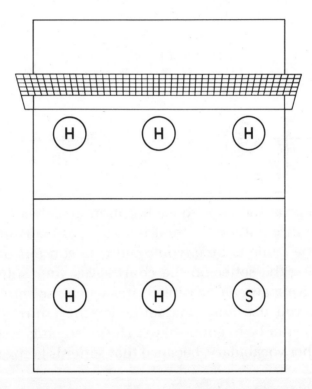

net, one of two options is used. The first is to convert to the four-two system and have the setter continue to feed the two hitters from the MF position. The second is to substitute for the setter at the net and for a hitter in the back row. The setter that normally rotates to the front row will be substituted for by a hitter and the hitter that would normally rotate to the back row will be substituted for by a setter *(see Figure 19)*.

FIGURE 19: THE REVOLVING DOOR—SUBSTITUTING IN THE FIVE-ONE

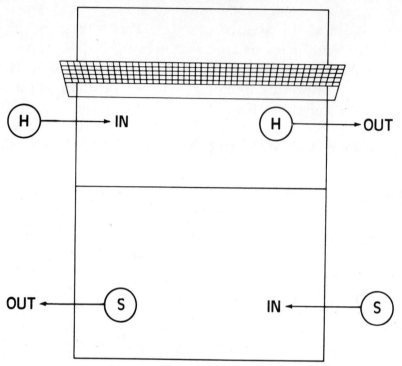

There are pros and cons to each option. It's always an advantage to have three hitters in the front row, but substitutions are limited. If the game is long, you're sure to run out of substitutions. Keeping the setter on the court saves your substitutions, but you're giving away a possible hitter when the setter is at the net. Also, if you use only one setter for the entire game, that person had better be in good shape. The word *fatigue* should not be in his or her vocabulary, because that setter is going to do a lot of work.

COVERING THE SPIKER

Once the ball has been set, the rest of the team must back up the spiker. If the spiker is blocked, everyone must be prepared to play the ball. This is done by pulling the whole team in around the hitter, forming a cup *(see Figure 20)*.

The players in the foreground have all closed around the hitter (#4) in case she is blocked.

Player Positions

How close these supporting players get to the hitter depends on a variety of circumstances. The first of these is the closeness of the set to the net. If the ball is right on the net, the chance of a block or a partial block is increased. The cup must move in closer. If the ball is well away from the net, the supporting player should adjust accordingly.

The hitters' tendencies will also influence where the cup forms. Hitters who hit low tend to get blocked straight down. Hitters attacking the ball higher tend to get blocked deeper in the court. A short hitter going up against taller blockers needs close support. A tall hitter going up against shorter blockers needs support further from the net. Short blockers tend to block soft, and the ball rebounds deeper into the court.

All players in these two photos are prepared to play the ball if the hitter is blocked. Notice how the male player in the middle ground has his hands up in order to play the ball with an overhand pass, while the two female players who have less reaction time are prepared to bump.

FIGURE 20: POSITIONS FOR COVERING THE SPIKER

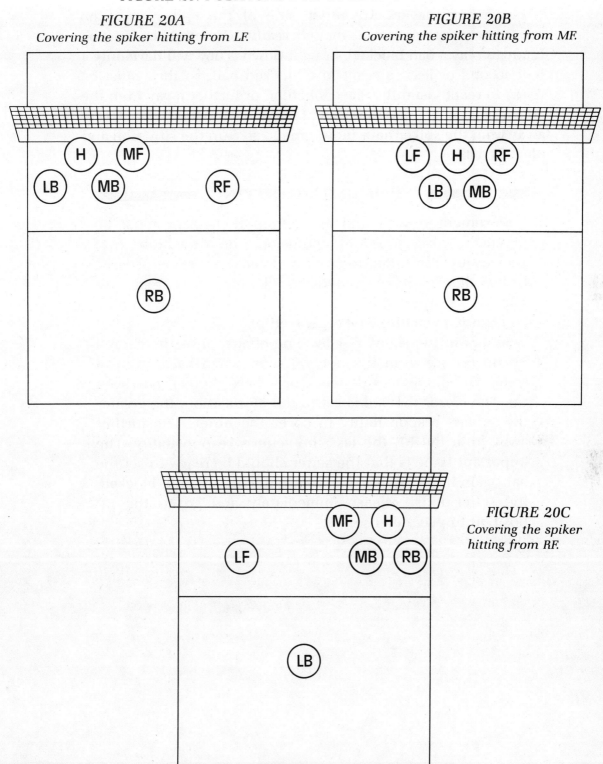

FIGURE 20A
Covering the spiker hitting from LF.

FIGURE 20B
Covering the spiker hitting from MF.

FIGURE 20C
Covering the spiker hitting from RF.

Technique

Supporting players on either side of the spiker must be squatting with their arms extended, ready to bump. They must be ready to play a ball blocked straight down. They will have only a half second or less to react to a blocked ball, so they must be ready to react instantly. Players behind or further away from the spiker need not squat; the normal ready position will do. Players away from the spiker have more time to size up the situation and play the ball.

TROUBLE SHOOTING

Movement toward and away from the spiker must be practiced. Also, to avoid confusion, the transition from backing up the hitter to playing defense must be orderly. Unless all team members understand their areas of responsibility, the result will look like feeding time at a cattle ranch instead of a smooth, well-organized play.

Setters in the six-two or five-one offense must be careful not to release from the net too soon when backing up a hitter. Of course, this depends on where the ball has been set. The closer the ball is set to the RF position, the greater the setter's responsibility to cover the hitter. The further away from the RF, the less the setter's responsibility. The important issue is that the setter should be ready to set the ball again if the hitter is blocked. If the hitter is not blocked, the setter must release immediately and go to the RB position to play defense.

7
DEFENSIVE STRATEGY: KEEPING THE BALL UP

As a famous trial lawyer put it, the defense never rests. Like basketball, soccer, and ice hockey, volleyball is a game of quick and unpredictable transition. There is no time to admire the quality of your last play. You must anticipate the upcoming play and take an appropriate position. If you snooze, you lose.

The defense is split roughly into two lines: the net players, who are eligible to block, and the back-row players, who must play up any ball that gets past the block.

BLOCKER'S RESPONSIBILITY

The best kind of defense is the type that doesn't allow the ball to come over the net to begin with. If the blockers can consistently keep the ball in the opponent's court, they deliver a crippling blow to the opponents and put the spikers under severe psychological strain. A hitter who is blocked tends to get rattled. Instead of whaling away on the ball and trying to hit past the block, the hitter begins to play it safe and dink or hit soft shots to the middle.

Each of the blockers has his or her own responsibility, namely, the blocker's opposite number at the net. Blockers should play one on one and not limit their blocking to the area of their position. Before each play begins, the front-line players should eyeball the eligible hitters and keep in mind what kind of offense the opponents are using. Use of a two-hitter offense usually rules out a middle hit, so the middle blocker can concentrate on which corner hitter will get the ball. The end blockers concentrate on the setter, each ready to block or drop off the net depending on where the set goes.

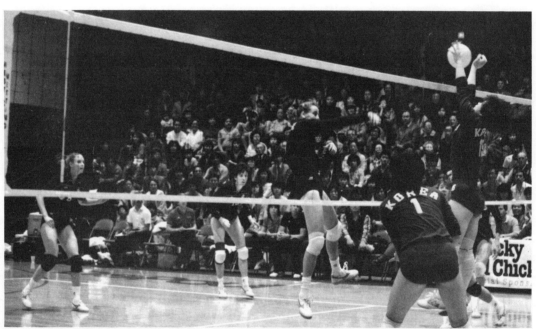

The middle blocker has beaten the spiker in a one-on-one situation.

Blocking a Three-Hitter Offense

The three-hitter offense complicates life for the blockers, especially the middle blocker. The middle blocker must guard against the quick hit, whether it is a one or a two set. If and when the middle hitter goes up, so does the middle blocker. It is the middle blocker's job to take away the straight-down power shot in the central area of the court. This area is most vulnerable, so the middle blocker must deliver the goods. Because of the nature of quick sets in the middle, the middle blocker can expect help only when the right or left blocker has keyed on a hitter and correctly diagnosed the play.

Blocking a Faked Set

If there is no set or the set is a fake, the middle blocker must be ready to move instantly. The ball will have been set to another player. The middle blocker must do the best possible job to close with the end blocker and get in on the block.

Positions

If every blocker has matched up properly with a spiker, each spiker will be faced with at least one blocker. Even if the opposition attempts to have two players hit out of the middle, they will be confronted by two blockers. When a corner hitter breaks for the middle, the opposite blocker tags right along. It's a philosophy of, "Whither thou goest, so also go I." If these one-on-one match-ups are properly maintained, a spiker simply cannot get free for an unblocked hit.

The end blockers are each responsible for positioning the corner block. Usually, the end blocker sets up opposite or just to the inside of the hitter to take away the line shot. The middle blocker, by closing the block, will take away the cross-court power shot.

The outside blocker should keep several things in mind when setting the block:

1. If the spiker has shown no ability to hit a line shot, the block should be set more to the inside. This will take away more of the cross-court angle and will make life easier for the diggers.
2. The outside blocker must angle his or her outside hand *in toward the court*. This prevents a hitter from wiping the ball off the block and out of bounds. If the ball strikes the blocker's outside hand, this hand position will turn it back into the area of play.
3. The outside blocker and the middle blocker must both be

vocal! If the hitter dinks, yell, "Dink!" If the ball is hit off the block, yell, "Touch!" The back-court players have problems of their own, and they can't always clearly see what is happening during your block. Communicate! Let your teammates know what is happening.

TRIPLE BLOCK

Occasionally, all the blockers get in on the same block. This block, called a triple block, usually happens in the middle. The middle blocker takes the central area away from the hitter as usual. The two end blockers close up, each taking a portion of the outside and seal off the angle shots.

In the rare event you have the opportunity or even the need to put up a triple block on an outside hitter, the outside blocker must anchor the block by taking away the line shot. If the hitter

A triple block; all front-row players have closed on and are reaching for the ball.

is so proficient as to necessitate a block by half the team, take away all the options you can. The other two blockers will take away the cross-court shots just by closing up. The block had better be successful. There are huge chunks of vacant territory along the net just begging for a dink.

BACK-LINE DEFENSE

Strictly speaking, there are only two defense postures for the back-line players, middle-up and middle-back. Both refer to the positioning of the middle back player.

Middle-Up and Middle-Back Defense

The middle-up defense is used chiefly against teams that dink often or just plain don't hit well. It positions the middle back player just to the inside of the block and about eight to ten feet behind it *(see Figure 21)*. The entire center area of the court and the area behind the block are the responsibility of the middle back.

FIGURE 21: MIDDLE-UP DEFENSE

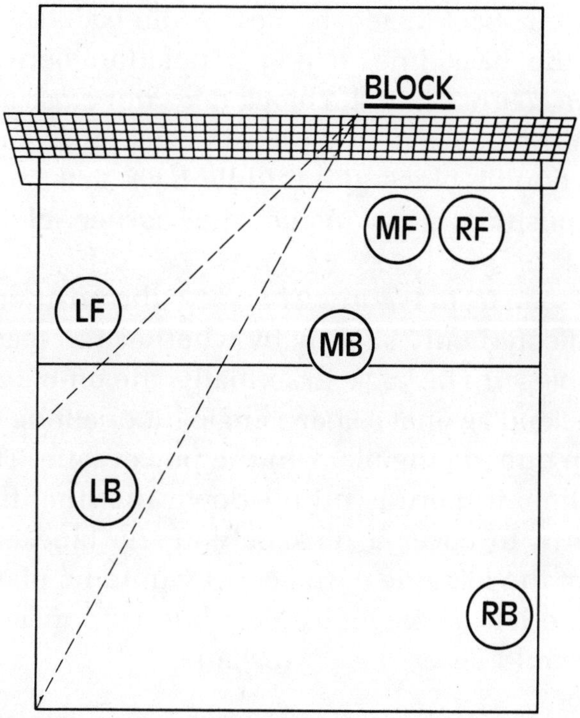

The block has not closed and the middle back is prepared to cover the hole.

In the middle-back defense, the middle back plays deep, just inside the the back line, taking a position between the two blockers *(see Figure 22)*. If the block does not close and the ball is hit between the blockers, the middle back must play the ball. If there is no double block, the middle back takes approximately the same position, just inside the corner blocker's inside shoulder.

As can be seen from Figures 21 and 22, the position of the other players is affected only slightly by whether the team plays with the middle back up or back. Essentially, the off-blocker drops off the net to defend against a sharp angle hit or a long dink. The left back sets up outside the block in the power lane. The right back covers the line; if there is no hit down the line, the right back must come in to cover a dink behind the blockers. An attack coming from the left side of the court would be played precisely opposite. The left back would have line responsibility, and the right back would cover the power lane.

FIGURE 22: MIDDLE-BACK DEFENSE

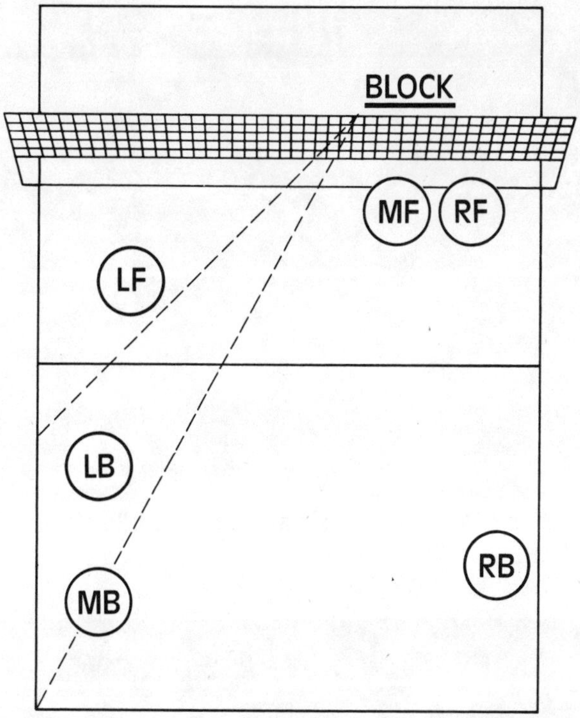

Adding Diggers

The middle-back defense also adds another digger to the power lane. As soon as the middle back sees that the block *will* close, he or she immediately moves toward the area of the power hit, just inside the block. This puts three players in the area to dig and still provides line cover.

Obviously, if you're up against a hot-hitting team, it is smart to have as many diggers as possible. On the other hand, if the other team is popping short hits and dinks into your undefended middle, adjust and have the middle play up.

Double Duty

The right and left backs are responsible for defending the line against spikes. They must also cover the area behind the blockers if the hitter dinks. This double duty is easier than it sounds. After the ball is set to an outside hitter, the respective back takes a

In this example, the block has closed and the middle back is playing just to the inside of the middle blocker.

Defending the line.

This player has placed herself perfectly. Foot on the line and just outside the block, with a full view of the hitter.

receiving or low-ready position in the back third of the court *(see Figure 23)*. Start with your outside foot on or just outside the sideline. Any ball above the height of your chest or head is going out; move right or left, but *get out of the way!* Don't accidentally touch the ball. Any ball beyond your outside foot is also out of bounds. Don't reach for anything to your left if you're playing left back; don't reach for anything to your right if you're the right back player. If the hitter is going to hit a line shot, you can generally see the hitter's shoulder drop and body rotate in your direction. Go to your dig position immediately and focus your attention.

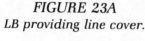

FIGURE 23: LINE COVER

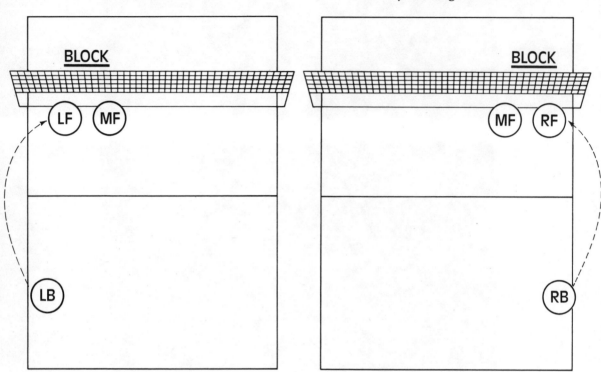

Many players take a slightly altered stance in playing the line. If you face your body in the direction of the hitter, your pass will be to the corner hitter playing in front of you, not to the setter. You can solve this problem by turning slightly toward the middle of the court. However, if the opposition's hitter dinks short and to the line, it will take you a little longer to come up. No problem. Carefully note each hitter's tendencies. Does he like to dink? Can she hit a line shot? If so, is it likely to be a vicious wallop or an easily passed, my-grandma-could-do-this wimp shot? Does he have a wipe shot? Each hitter must be played according to his or her tendencies and talent. Don't try to play them all the same way.

If the block takes the line shot away or you can see that there will be no line shot, begin circling in behind the blockers. Don't lose sight of the hitter. If the hitter has been concealed by the block, go to the outside until you can see the hitter again. It's easier to see what they're doing than to guess. Stay on the balls of your feet, ready to play up a dink or a ball that comes off the block. If you're not involved in the play, you should end up about four feet behind and just to the outside of the outside blocker's shoulder. The path you have taken—an arc—should keep you properly positioned throughout the play.

Digging Power Shots

The defensive back kitty-corner from each of the opposing corner spikers is the player most likely to be called on to dig a power shot. This means the right back will cover a cross-court shot coming from the left corner; the left back covers a cross-court shot coming from the right corner.

The technique for coverage is the same for both. Once the set is made, the back must take a position two or three feet inside the inside shoulder of the block. You should be four to six feet from

Both players in the foreground have their weight forward and are ready to react to the spike.

the sideline and just in front of the back third of the court *(see Figure 24)*.

Keep your eyes on the hitter. The angle of the hitter's spiking shoulder and arm will tell you where the ball is going. You may have to adjust left or right slightly. Get into a crouch or receiving position, arms at the ready, weight on the balls of your feet or even further forward, on your toes. You must get well under the ball to make a good dig. Many players take a full squat and slap the floor with the palms of their hands to get *down* and get *ready*. You must have strong desire and quickness to keep the ball off the floor. The time between when the hitter puts a stamp on the ball and air-mails it to you and when it arrives is something less than one-half second.

FIGURE 24: COVERING CROSS-COURT SHOTS

FIGURE 24A
LB covering power lane.

FIGURE 24B
RB covering power lane.

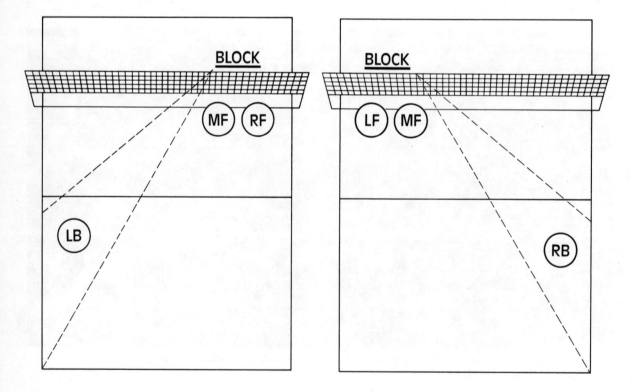

Each hitter has tendencies in hitting a power shot. Some hit long, others hit short. Some have a blistering, peel-the-paint-off-the-floor hard spike. Others can boast only that the ball stayed in bounds, even if the digger did laugh as the ball was played. Some can get high enough to hit almost straight down; most can't. Don't make the beginner's mistake of charging the net in anticipation of a dig. Hold your position unless you are absolutely sure the hitter is going to angle the ball sharply down. It is more common to be out of position because you're in too deep rather than back too far.

If the spike is high, at chest level, don't panic and jump at it. You merely have to straighten your legs in order to get both arms on the ball. If the ball is head high or better, remember where you are in relation to the sideline. Unless the ball is coming down faster than a bad stock on a Friday afternoon, it is probably out of bounds. Let it go.

Although the floor positions and digging techniques are the same for both the outside defensive backs, the left back has a slightly more difficult assignment. The left back must play against the opposition's strong side hitter. You may have to make adjustments, such as pushing up two feet or so to get a better position on the strong side hitter. Some teams may wish to switch and put their best digger at the left back position. Additional support may be gained from having the middle back and the off-blocker, the outside hitter not involved in the block, pinch in toward the left back.

Off-Blocker's Role

The off-blocker is responsible for very sharp angle spikes that the hitter may try to cut between the net and the ten-foot line. The off-blocker must also cover dinks to the center area near the net. The off-blocker's usual position is about three or four feet from the sideline and just inside the ten-foot line *(see Figure 25)*.

Unless you can plainly see by the hitter's body language that there will be no hit to your area, you should take the usual dig position. Keep your eye on the hitter's shoulder. It is a key for all digging. If the hitter's body rotates sharply and almost seems to point at you, get down and get ready! You're about to be tested.

If you plainly see that the hitter is not going to spike, straighten your legs slightly but keep your weight forward on the balls of your feet. You may have to play up a dink or a touch off the block.

FIGURE 25: OFF-BLOCKER'S POSITION

FIGURE 25A
Position of off-blocker, left side.

FIGURE 25B
Position of off-blocker, right side.

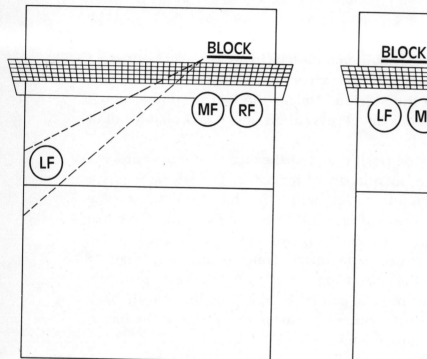
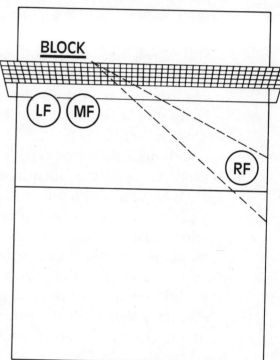

As with digging in any position, you must get under the ball to make a decent pass. Always try to bear in mind your position on the court relative to the sideline. If you're in the squat position three feet from the sideline and the ball is at head level, get out of the way; the ball is going out of bounds.

DIFFICULT BALLS

Balls that are difficult to dig fall into three categories: those hit to the digger's side, those that are high, and those that are short.

Correctly handling each of these requires distinctly different techniques.

Ball Hit to the Digger's Side

Balls hit to the digger's side, either right or left, are probably the easiest of the three to handle. So long as the position you've taken is not terribly off, you can still make the save, provided you have taken the proper stance and the ball is no more than two or three feet from you.

Stepping out to make a difficult save.

Technique. Step out, leading with the foot nearest the ball. Push off with the foot furthest from the ball. Keep low. Your weight should be shifting as you make contact with the ball from the push-off foot to the step-out foot. Get both arms under the ball if possible. If it's not possible get one arm under the ball.

Under no circumstances should you take your eyes off the ball even for an instant. This requires total concentration. Look the ball in and look the ball out.

After you make contact, make no attempt to break your fall. Just allow your body to relax, and go to the floor on your derriere, allowing your momentum to rock you off the floor and almost to your shoulders. *Do not do a backward somersault.* This is an easy, graceful movement. It does not require rolling yourself into a ball and risking injury to your neck and spine. You should be relatively close to the floor in the digging position, so dropping to the floor and rocking on your back will give your body no great shock. Because your momentum is to the side, you will finish this movement sideways to your original position.

Drill. Practice stepping out with a partner in the same manner as you practiced initially for spikes. First return balls hit slowly, then increase the speed of the hits as the motion grows more natural.

Strategy. Most people find that they can go to one side more easily than to the other. Right-handed people move better to their left; left-handed people move better to their right. That's because when you walk or run, the dominant foot is planted and helps get your body in motion. The nondominant foot takes the first step. You can compensate for this tendency by giving a *little* more room to the hitter on the side you move to more easily. Right-handed diggers should give the hitter more room on the left; left-handed diggers should give the hitter more room on the right. This "cheating" to the dominant side will help you cover more territory and cover it more adeptly.

Ball Hit High

All players, sooner or later, are faced with the awesome threat of the much dreaded *six-pack*, i.e., being hit in the face with the ball. The term originated in California. An enterprising team captain decided to motivate his fellow players by offering a free six-pack of beer to any hitter who could blast a digger in the face or head with the ball. The results, unfortunately, have been lost to posterity.

This player on the United States Women's team has straightened her legs slightly to play a ball that will be arriving shortly.

When a ball is coming at you high, one sure way to save your face is to move it out of the way. That, however, does not solve your problem if the ball is in bounds. There are two ways to play a ball coming at you high. The first has already been discussed; simply straighten your legs. If the resulting bump goes to the setter, well and good. Many times however, the bump will come off your arms and go straight back over the net, especially if the ball is coming down fast.

Peek-a-Boo or Suicide Bump. Another and perhaps better way to play a ball coming toward your face is the peek-a-boo or suicide bump. By bending your arms at the elbow and bringing your joined hands back toward your face you can bump the ball with the underside of your hands. If you open your hands slightly but keep your thumbs together, you will be able to keep your eyes on the ball until you make contact. You can adjust your position in relation to the ball by straightening your legs if you must or by falling gently backward and using the rocking motion described in the step-out dig to absorb the impact of going to the floor.

Advantages. There are advantages in using the peek-a-boo bump. It uses a player's natural reflex to protect the face, so it's easy to learn and the reaction time is very fast. By taking the basic ready position, you have already joined your hands. It is quite simple to bring them up in front of you.

Second, you do not lose sight of the ball. You can sight the ball right into your hands by using split vision. It is also noteworthy that a player jumping up suddenly to play a high ball may end up off balance during or after the bump. This loss of balance can affect a player's concentration. That is less likely to happen when using this technique.

Ball Hit Short

The most difficult kind of ball to get to quickly is the ball that is hit short of your position. In a low position, it's much easier to move sideways or even backward than to move forward.

If the ball is only a foot or two in front of you, you can play it by taking a short, quick step forward with your dominant foot and dropping the knee of that foot to the floor. This will help to provide a stable base. Plant the nondominant foot and, with your arms close to the floor, reach for the ball and bump it. Remember, you must get *under* the ball. Many players like to wear knee pads to guard against bruising in a play like this.

A dive.

DIVING

More advanced players may wish to learn the fine art of diving. In covering dinks, short shots, or just plain errant passes, a dive can cover a lot of court. In some situations it is the only way to save the ball. This book doesn't cover diving because it is dangerous and should be taught under the close tutelage of someone who knows what he or she is doing.

Even then, it must be approached slowly and by graduated steps. Care must be taken to avoid injury. Five or six stitches may close up a split chin (a common injury), but the psychological impact of getting hurt may remain long after the wound has healed. If you injure yourself diving, you're certainly going to be reluctant to put yourself in jeopardy the next time. By all means, learn how to dive. But learn it under the supervision of a qualified instructor you trust.

Do or die! One of the players on the Japanese National Women's team is already on the floor.

8
FUN UNDER THE SUN: PLAYING BEACH BALL

The origin of beach volleyball is cloaked in lore, mystery, and the mists of time. Depending on your point of view and who's telling the story, it was originated by the legendary citizens of Atlantis and kept alive after the demise of that unfortunate continent by the priesthood of a secret cult that worshipped the sun. Or, it was given to man- (and woman-) kind at the direction of an apparition, blond-haired and clothed in a white Speedo, on the shores of distant Avalon as a diversion for knights recovering from knee surgery.

BEACH VOLLEYBALL RULES

Beach volleyball differs from the indoor game in many important respects. The most striking is that there are only two players on a side, although the court dimensions and the height of the net are the same as for indoors. The side and end lines are marked with rope if possible; if rope is unavailable, it is permissible on many beaches to draw lines in the sand. Since there is no center line, there is no center-line violation as long as a player does not interfere with an opponent.

The ball is heavier than the standard ball and is of 18-piece construction. The extra weight keeps the ball a bit steadier in the wind. The ball is usually a little underinflated as well, making it less responsive to a spike or a bump.

Blocking is permitted by either of the partners as long as the vertical plane of the net is not broken. *There is no blocking over the net.* A player may recontact the ball following a block, but both contacts count toward the maximum of three touches. A player who contacts the net is honor-bound to call the foul. Likewise, custom dictates that players call all their own fouls whether there is a referee or not.

Unlike United States Volleyball Association rules that call for a "dead ball" after below-the-waist contact, a ball striking any bodily appendage is sometimes considered to be in play in beach volleyball. However, Midwest rules dictate below-the-waist contact is illegal.

Usually, there is no more than one official for beach ball. This ref keeps score and calls lines and fouls. In a game to 11 points, the ref indicates a change of sides after every four points scored (2–2, 3–1, 6–2, 5–3, etc.). In a game to 15, this switching of courts occurs every five points scored (3–2, 4–1, 6–4, 8–2, etc.). This neutralizes any advantage on one side of the court due to wind or sun. Two time-outs are allowed per game. These may be requested any time the ball is dead. There are no substitutions. However, unlimited requests for time to stretch out leg cramps are honored, as well as time to brush off sand.

Rules for Serving

Players must keep the same serving order during the game. The serve is allowed from *any* point behind the end line. There are no overlaps, and players may play either side of the court at any time during the game.

Rules for Setting

Setting is allowed *directly* in front of or behind the setter only. Setting off to the setter's right or left side is not permitted. Many players set using a low bump pass to avoid mishandling the heavier outdoor ball.

Rules for Hitting

An open-hand dink is not allowed, but hitting the ball using the off-speed topspin shot is, as is hitting the ball with the knuckles of a fist. This "cobra shot" is generally used to place the ball deep in the opponent's court, especially over or past a block.

Rules for Defense

Generally, it is not permissible to receive a serve using the overhand set. As in indoors, the bump must be used. However, odd as it may seem, it is considered perfectly acceptable to dig a spike using the set as long as it's done clearly, *even if successive contact with the ball occurs*. This double hit is legal as long as it constitutes one attempt to play the ball. Similarly, using a single open hand to play a hard-driven ball is allowed. This lenient interpretation of the rules gives the defense an advantage and leads to longer volleys. It also keeps things more exciting for the spectators.

Playing volleyball on the beach leads to the best of times and the worst of times. Digging a ball is easier outside than inside. Sand is soft; it has plenty of give and cushions your movement. You can dive for a ball outdoors that you would never go after indoors. Floorburns hurt! On the sand you can literally throw your body around with almost reckless abandon.

On the other hand, because sand is soft and cushions your movement, it is tougher to jump out of. You will lose a few inches from your indoor jump. For players who are 6'3" that's no big deal, but shorter players will need to make a serious adjustment. In addition, because you will be hitting a heavier ball that is deliberately kept underinflated, your spike will lose speed and impact. The advantage definitely belongs to the defense.

BEACH BALL STRATEGY

Serving

The addition of sun and wind to the game makes passing the ball a new challenge; many servers like to use a "sky ball," especially if the sun is directly overhead. The sky-ball serve is hit underhand and should soar up into the heavens as high as possible. It can be difficult to see, let alone pass. Floaters served into the wind or with the wind also take on new characteristics that can make them difficult to play up. The topspin serve can be a particularly troublesome ball to field, especially when hit into the wind. The wind resistance magnifies the effect of the top spin on the ball and causes it to take a sudden and almost violent dive. But beware of using this serve with the wind behind you. In that case, the wind will tend to hold the ball up and cause it to sail.

As with serving indoors, target the area you wish to serve: the seam between your opponents, deep into the corners, a weak passer, a weak hitter, or a player who is tiring. If you are serving with the wind at your back, it is wise to keep the ball in the middle of the opponent's court. A serve down the line or to the end line may be pushed out of bounds by the wind.

Defensive Strategy

After the serve, both players should take a defensive position about 20 feet or so from the net and toward the middle of the court. From there, defensive position depends on the set and the hitter. A close set may require one partner to block and the other to cover for a dig. A set far from the net may require both players to stay back for a dig or one to play up for a cobra shot and the other to stay deep.

Remember to key on the spiker's approach and the proximity of the set to the net. A deep set generally calls for the defense to pull back from the net. The further the set is from the net, the less the vertical angle the spiker can achieve at the moment of impact. The closer the set is to the net, the greater the verical angle probably will be. A close set will require the defense to come in closer for a more straight-down shot.

As indoors, keep in mind a hitter's tendencies. Most people have favorite shots and favorite places on the court to hit to. It is an unusual beach that doesn't have a waiting list to play the winners. Use waiting time to scout your opponents.

Setting Strategy

One nice thing about setting on the beach is that you almost never have to call for the ball that your partner just passed. If you don't play the ball, no one is left to help you out. As soon as your partner indicates by voice or body position that he or she will pass the incoming ball, break for the net. If the pass is off, only you can make the save, and you will have to react instantly to get to the ball.

One player passes as his partner races to the net to set.

Where to Set. Ideally, the ball is passed to and set from the midpoint of the net and one and a half to three feet back from it. The set must be high enough to allow the spiker time to get to the ball. It must be close enough to allow the hitter a good vertical angle. However, the set cannot be so close and so high that the opponents have time and opportunity to set up a good block.

Keep in mind the effect of the wind on the set. Is the wind

Even though the ball is low, this player has his hands up and is ready to set. His knees are bent to allow him to get under the ball as fully as possible.

strong enough and the ball high enough that the ball will be blown over the net to set the other side?

From what area of the court did your partner just pass the ball? The closer the two of you were to begin with, the less time your partner needs to approach the set. The greater the distance, the greater the area your partner must cover and the higher the set must be to allow for a good approach.

What is the opposition doing? Are both of them back, enabling you to put the ball "right on" for your partner? Or is one of them at the net, ready to block? In that case, you must keep the set a little further back from the net. Don't break your concentration, but don't lose your awareness either.

Planning Ahead. Most partners agree before a match what general area will be set. Almost no one uses a back set. On some beaches, back sets are frowned on; on others, a back set that goes over the net untouched by your partner is a foul. Because the sand is so difficult to move through and take off from, quick hits, ones, and twos are the exception, not the rule. These plays can be and sometimes are used, but if you and your partner have 900 square feet of undefended sand *behind* you, you may have to do some very fancy—and fast—footwork just to cover up.

Being Consistent. A great many beach pairs set each other directly over the setter's head. This keeps every play consistent, and the hitter always knows where the set will be. There is no waiting to see where the setter will put the ball. It also removes the possibility of verbal signals being misunderstood or just plain not heard. Crowd noise and the sound of the surf can make conversation difficult in the heat of the game. If the pass is to the mid-area of the net and the set is in the same place, the hitter has an excellent view of what the defense is doing, as well as a wide range of hitting angles.

Getting Ready. After the set, drop off the net, backing quickly to a defensive position. Don't become a spectator! Hard-driven balls that are dug frequently come back over the net immediately. Stay in the play and be ready to react should you have to chase down a ball returned deep to your own court. The spiker will have little or no opportunity to play up a quickly returned ball.

Spiking on the Beach

The person who spikes the ball has the unenviable responsibility to move as quickly as possible in loose, unstable sand, take the usual approach in same aforementioned medium, and then explode out of this cushiony stuff to beat the ball down into the opponent's court. Jumping out of sand requires all the strength and drive a player can bring to bear. But there are compensations. You will have a full 900 square feet of court to hit into. And there are only two persons to defend all that miniature Sahara. Should you be confronted by a block, it will only be one person deep. You can cut around a block or use a closed-fist cobra shot to poke around it.

Good follow-through, a nice jump, and the smile on the setter's face tell you the result of this spike.

Technique. Just as jumping on the beach requires all your strength, so will hitting the ball. With the ball's heavier weight and unresponsiveness, you must really generate some force to hit a good spike. But the technique for hitting is the same. Concentrate totally on the ball as you begin your jump. Try to be aware of the position the players on the other side have taken. When you hit the ball, explode on it as forcefully as you can, remembering to get your hand over the top of the ball to impart top spin just as you would indoors.

Try to place the ball to the right, left, or in front of a particular opponent. If you notice one of them is playing short, stroke the ball past that player. A placed hit is much more likely to succeed than a ball that is just spiked over blindly.

The beginning of this play was a bad pass; note where the setter is standing. But effort and communication have turned disaster into a decent play.

Cobra Shot. The cobra shot, or beach dink, should be used only under the following conditions:

1. The ball has been poorly set and is going over the net or is being blown over the net.
2. The set is close to the net and/or the blocker has you well covered.
3. Your opponents have set up much too close to the net, leaving miles of undefended micro-Mojave behind them.
4. You are hitting with all the explosive force and accuracy of a pound of fettucine that has been marinating in seawater for a full week.

Although dinking is not allowed on the beach, a roll shot is similar to a dink but is done with the fist closed. The strategy is the same as for dinking indoors. Put the ball where your opponents aren't. You have a lot of room to work with, so take advantage of it.

Landing. In taking an approach to hit or in making a tip-over shot, you do not have to worry about flying through the air or broad jumping. There is no line-foul violation if you come down under the net or even on the other side. This ruling is particularly handy when you're trying to make a flying save. So long as you don't interfere with an opponent or touch the net, you don't have to be bothered with the consequences of where you'll come down after you hit the ball.

Blocking on the Beach

Blocking in beach volleyball is a risky business. While it is permitted and many players can use it effectively, blocking is not the same weapon on the beach that it is indoors. You cannot reach across the net to block. That takes a lot of leverage away from the defenders. The attacker also is allowed to wipe the ball off the blocker's hands. This tactic can be especially useful because if the blocker closes completely with the net, he or she has committed a foul.

Many players refrain from blocking unless their opponents are setting very close to the net on a regular basis. Using the block may force the opponents to set further away from the net. Blocking technique for beach ball does not vary much from indoors except that the arms must go straight up instead of angling across the net. Timing may be affected slightly because of the difficulty of getting out of the sand. The sand will definitely limit the height of the jump.

The blocker must take away the spiker's favorite shot, either cross-court or line. The digger must react to the block and cover the open shot. Should the blocker deflect the ball, the digger should react likewise. If the blocker can reach a self-deflected ball, he or she should place it up into the air as high as possible. The next shot *must* go over the net; a block counts as one of the

The block is up, but will it be good? The hitter appears to be cutting towards the blocker's left shoulder. The man playing back is attempting to adjust.

three allowable touches of the ball. The extra hang time may give your partner the time needed to make the play.

HOW TO WIN

Teams should try to pair up so that they have opposite, not mutual talents. Good hitters should team up with good setters, good diggers with good blockers, and so on. Usually one player takes on the primary responsibility of playing up the serve.

It is especially important to call for the ball on the beach. A loudly called "Mine!" lets your partner know you will pass the ball, your partner will set, and you will hit. A ball that is close to the line should be called in or out by the partner *not* playing the ball; the person playing the ball can only guess where the line is. A call of "I'm down" tells your partner you will not be able to play the next ball following a save. "I'm up" tells your partner that you can.

There is only one way to win in beach volleyball. Be in great physical shape and master all phases of the game—pass, set, hit, dig, and serve. A tremendous amount of stamina is needed, especially in one- or two-day tournaments. To compete success- fully, you must build your stamina and have the willpower to keep going even when you're physically exhausted. The final game of a tournament is frequently held in mid-afternoon when the temperature is hottest. Your endurance will be tested severely.

Playing a close one. Both players attempt to block a ball that has been set too near the net.

A player who is deficient in any phase of the game is quickly found out, and the opponents will key accordingly. The weaker passer or spiker will be served to. A tiring player will find the opponents playing the ball more frequently to his or her side. A poor digger will be spiked to. The only real specialists in beach volleyball are those who prefer the right side over the left side of the court and vice versa. There is no place to hide on the beach.

When you practice, always play against the best competition you can find, and play as hard and well as you can. The only way to build endurance is by enduring. You must push yourself beyond your self-conceived physical limits to build your stamina. Play every game as though it were the deciding match of a tournament.

PROFESSIONAL BEACH VOLLEYBALL

Until 1976, beach players competed only for the pleasure of being number one and occasionally for the responsibility of a new trophy to dust. However, by 1981 sponsors had donated an attractive amount of money toward prizes for the World Championship of Volleyball, an event that has attracted 15,000 spectators. A professional tour has also been organized, with events stretching from Hermosa Beach, California, to Fort Lauderdale, Florida. The tour also was hosted by such famous beach cities as Chicago and Scottsdale, Arizona. In the 1985 season, the top money-earner on the tour, Mike Dodd, made $32,860. Not a bad piece of change for running around and having fun.

APPENDIX:
WHO TO CONTACT

UNITED STATES VOLLEYBALL ASSOCIATION

National Commissioner: Rebecca Howard
891 Southwood Drive
Littleton, CO 80121
(303) 794-7720

Regions

ALASKA REGION (Alaska)

Commissioner: Virgil Hooe
5020 Fairbanks St.
Anchorage, AK 99503
(907) 338-2269 (Home)
(907) 563-3811 (Bus.)

ALOHA REGION (Hawaii, except Island of Hawaii)

Commissioner: Frederick D. Hiapo
1546 Hanai Loop
Honolulu, HI 96817
(808) 847-3196

CAROLINA REGION (North Carolina and South Carolina)
Commissioner: Fred Wendelboe
4240 Briar Creek Road
Clemmons, NC 27012
(919) 766-5075

CHESAPEAKE REGION (Delaware, Maryland, Washington, D.C., and Virginia)
Commissioner: Richard E. Smith
14627 National Dr.
Chantilly, VA 22012
(703) 968-7270

COLUMBIA EMPIRE REGION (Oregon)
Commissioner: David Soderquist
3431 S.E. 10th
Portland, OR 97202
(503) 235-2520

CORNBELT REGION (Iowa)
Regional Commissioner: Sandy Hansen
6770 NW Trail Ridge Drive
Johnston, Iowa 50131
(515) 278-1912

DELTA REGION (Arkansas, Louisiana, Mississippi, and Western Tennessee)
Commissioner: Carl Roberts
305 Stonewall Dr.
Jacksonville, AR 72076
(501) 982-1269

EVERGREEN REGION (Washington, Northern Idaho, and Montana)
Commissioner: Joyce M. Johnson
7929 N.E. 175th
Bothell, WA 98011
(206) 486-5047 (Home)
(206) 365-6161 (Bus.)

FLORIDA REGION (Florida & U.S. Islands of the Caribbean)

Commissioner: Mark Headrick
240-08 Moreeloop
Winter Springs, FL 32708
(305) 327-0224

GARDEN-EMPIRE REGION (New Jersey and New York)

Comissioner: Mark Hatten
10 Penrose Lane
Piscataway, NJ 08854
(201) 463-3379 (Home)
(201) 231-8211 (Bus.)

GREAT LAKES REGION (Illinois)

Commissioner: Lea Wagner
9124 W. Hollyberry
Des Plaines, IL 60016
(312) 297-3419

GREAT PLAINS REGION (Nebraska)

Commissioner: Marge Davenport
Route 13
Lincoln, NE 68527
(402) 488-9109

HEART OF AMERICA REGION (Kansas and Missouri)

Commissioner: Bonnie Schannuth
5501 Rockhill Rd.
Kansas City, MO 64110
(816) 333-9027

INTERMOUNTAIN REGION (Utah, Nevada, and Southern Idaho)

Associate Commissioner for Utah: Julie Morgan University of Utah
Special Events Center
Salt Lake City, UT 84112
(801) 581-6843 (Home)
(801) 278-1549

IROQUOIS EMPIRE REGION (New York, except Metro City & Long Island)

Commissioner: The Rev. Charles K. Dwyer
49 Killean Park,
Albany, NY 12205
(Res) (518) 869-6417

KEYSTONE REGION (Pennsylvania, except Western Border Counties)

Commissioner: Jack Newns
3546 Gloucester Lanes
Philadelphia, PA 19114
(215) 824-0533 (Home)
(201) 532-2915/2516 (Bus.)

LAKELAND REGION (Wisconsin and Upper Michigan)

Commissioner: Dave Dickens
6217 Putnam Road
Madison, WI 53713
(608) 271-6376

LONE STAR REGION (South Texas)

Commissioner: W. L. "Will" Vick
7926 Sturdy Oaks Drive
San Antonio, TX 78233
(512) 653-4327 (Home)
(512) 652-4374 (Bus.)

MICHIANA REGION (Michigan and Indiana)

President (Commissioner)/Treasurer: Charles A. Stemm
29089 U.S. 20 W
Suite A-10
Elkhart, IN 46514
(219) 295-6110

MOKU O KEAWE REGION (Island and County of Hawaii)

Commissioner: Elroy T. L. Osorio
15 Laimana St.
Hilo, HI 96720
(808) 961-6279 (Home)
935-2816 (Bus.)

NEW ENGLAND REGION (Maine, New Hampshire, Vermont, Massachusetts, Rhode Island, and Connecticut)

Commissioner: David A. Castanon
21 Castano Ct.
Needham, MA 02173
(617) 449-5696

NORTH COUNTRY REGION (Minnesota, North Dakota, and South Dakota)

Commissioner: Jake Lacis
6708 Idaho Ave N.
Brooklyn Park, MN 55428
(612) 533-4776

NORTHERN CALIFORNIA REGION (Northern California)

Commissioner: Chris Stanley
643 30th St.
Richmond, CA 94804
(415) 642-9412 (Home)
(415) 237-8382 (Bus.)

OHIO VALLEY REGION (West Virginia, Ohio, Kentucky, and Border Counties of Pennsylvania)

Commissioner: Roland I. Stone
P.O. Box 24,
Coraopolis, PA 15108
(412) 262-1904

ROCKY MOUNTAIN REGION (Colorado and Wyoming)

Commissioner-Registar (Pres.):   Fran Zelinkoff
3201 S. Magnolia St.
Denver, CO 80224
(303) 758-6723

SOUTHERN REGION (Alabama, Georgia, Tennessee, except Memphis)

President (Commissioner):   Bill Fulford
P.O. Box 1006
Gadsden, AL 35902
(205) 547-4947

SOUTHERN CALIFORNIA REGION (Southern California)

Corporation Office: Southern California Volleyball Association
2008 West Carson Street
Suite #207
Torrance, CA 90501
(213) 320-9440

Commissioner/President: Ted Mueller
16699 Demaret Place
Granada Hills, CA 90501
(213) 360-3721

SUN COUNTRY REGION (Arizona, New Mexico, and West Texas)

Commissioner & President, Board of Directors: Fred Buehler
c/o Intramurals/Recrea-
tion Services, UT
El Paso, TX 79968
(915) 747-5112

TEXOMA REGION (North Texas and Oklahoma)

Commissioner: Nancy Strader
Route 1, Box 495A
S Houston School Road
Lancaster, TX 75146
(214) 223-1143
(214) 223-4717

ARMED FORCES JAPAN SUBREGION

Commissioner: Gene R. Newman
500 M.I. Group
APO San Francisco 96343
(Military) (233) 5252/6738

S. AIR FORCE

mmissioner: Steve Ducoff
8234 Phoenix
Universal City, TX 78148
(512) 658-1486 (Home)
(512) 652-3471 (Bus.)

U.S. AIR FORCE EUROPE

District Commissioner: CMSgt Charles A. Pietrowski
Box 4086
APO New York 09009

U.S. ARMY

Commissioner: George Garrett
HQDA (DAAG—MSP)
Alexandria, VA 22331
(703) 325-9715

U.S. ARMY EUROPE

Commissioner: Micheal Paguia, MSA
Sports Heidelberg
APO NY 09102

OUTDOOR VOLLEYBALL (BEACH AND GRASS TOURNAMENT INFORMATION)

ALABAMA

Information: Tommy Roberts
1642 B Sneed Road
Montgomery, AL 36115
(205) 272-5952

CALIFORNIA

San Rafael: San Rafael Recreation Department
(415) 456-1112

CALIFORNIA (cont.)

Irvine: Mike Puritz
           (714) 856-7218

Whittier: Whittier-Rio Hondo Kiwanis Club
             Ray Corman
             (213) 693-7183

More information: Joel Budgor
                     (415) 465-1426

                     Chris Stanley
                     (418) 73V-BALL

COLORADO:

MSC Tournaments: Pat Johnson
                    (303) 423-2234

Aspen City Limits Tournaments: Tim Weland
                                  641 S. Washington
                                  Denver, CO 80209
                                  (303) 744-0489
                                  (303) 377-2701

Boulder: Boulder Parks and Recreation Department
            P.O. Box 791
            Boulder, CO 80306
            (303) 441-3422

Denver: Rick's Cafe
           80 S. Madison
           Denver, CO 80209
           (303) 399-4448

Fort Collins: Fort Collins Parks and Recreation Department
                 145 E. Mountain
                 Fort Collins, CO 80521
                 (303) 221-6640

Fort Morgan: Brian Grennan
                507 Southridge Road
                Fort Morgan, CO 80701

Lakewood: Bob Schmitz
              (303) 987-7840

Pike's Peak Special Olympics: Nell Utz
                                  (303) 633-4601
                                  (303) 473-4878

Steamboat Springs: Susan Sommer
                       (303) 879-4300

Vail: Vail Recreation Department
          75 S. Frontage Road
          Vail, CO 81657
          (303) 476-2040

Winter Park: Mike Wirsing
                 (303) 726-8501

ILLINOIS
Information: AA Sports, Inc.
                3544 N. Southport
                Chicago, IL 60657
                (312) 472-8171
                (800) 772-6142 (outside Illinois)

INDIANA
Information: Brad Wade
                R.R. #4
                Green Acres
                Loogootee, IN 47553
                (812) 295-4229

MICHIGAN
Grand Haven: Charles Holleman
                 (616) 846-1116

Lansing: Dan Kitchell
             (517) 372-2204

Muskegon: Kevin David
              (616) 759-7894

MICHIGAN (cont.)

South Haven: Dene Hadden
779 Phoenix Street
South Haven, MI 49090

OREGON-WASHINGTON

Information: Brock Olson
Corvalis
(503) 683-8625

Olympia: Mark Schmidt
(206) 943-2823

Seaside: Steve Hinton
(503) 738-7134
(800) 452-6740 (in Oregon)

PENNSYLVANIA

Information: Earthworms Volleyball Club
Johnstown
Don Civis
(814) 536-3028

Denny Cruise
(814) 255-5543

Meadville Recreation Authority
(814) 724-6006

SOUTH CAROLINA

Information: Margy Beckmeyer
14 Spyglass Dr.
Aiken, SC 29801
(803) 648-8223

Windjammer tournaments: Joel Wolf
(803) 883-3440

Cliff Rios
(803) 886-5262

TENNESSEE

Nashville: Ken Debelak
               7201 Patten Lane
               Nashville, TN 37221
               (615) 646-5362
               (615) 322-2099

Murfreesboro: Glenn Hanley
                  (615) 755-4222

Chattanooga: Tony Jadin
                 (615) 755-4222

TEXAS

Information: Splendor in the Grass
                Volleyball Association
                A. M. Marquez
                2211 N. Henderson
                Dallas, TX 75206
                (214) 827-2716

VERMONT

Information: W. R. Jopling
                Road 3, Box 3400
                Montpelier, VT 05602
                (802) 229-5960

SUPPLIES AND EQUIPMENT

AA Sports, Inc.
3544 N. Southport
Chicago, IL 60657
(312) 472-8171

AA Silkscreening
Team Outfitting and
Silkscreening Services
(312) 472-4286

Sports Camps International
734 Alger S.E.
Grand Rapids, MI 49507
(800) 253-6074 (outside Michigan)
(800) 632-8654

GLOSSARY

Antenna: The vertical rods attached along the outside edge of the net to mark the widest extension of the court. A ball touching an antenna is *out of bounds.*

Attack: The offensive action of hitting the ball into the opponents' court.

Attack block: An attempt by a defensive player or players to intercept the ball after the *spiker* has hit it, and force the ball to the floor before it crosses the net.

Attack line: The in-court line, ten feet from the net, that separates front-row hitters from back-row players. Back-row players may not jump to attack the ball in front of this boundary.

Backhand dig: Contacting the ball with the back of the hand to make a save.

Back set: A set made to a hitter behind the *setter.*

Beach dig: Receiving a *spike* with open hands and directing the ball upward; allowed *only* in beach play and maybe not even then. Local rules or traditions may apply.

Block: A defensive play by one or more defensive players designed to intercept a spiked ball at or near the net.

Bump pass: Use of the joined forearms to pass the ball underhand.

164

Bump set: Use of the *bump pass* to place the ball where a hitter can attack it.

Center line: The boundary that runs under the net and divides the court into two equal halves. It is a *foul* to cross the center line completely while the ball is in play.

Coldcock: An unexpected, one-punch attack on an individual, usually coming from behind. It's not a nice thing to do, and that's why this word is not used anywhere in this book.

Contacted ball: A ball that brushes or touches any part of a player's body or clothes.

Cross-court serve: A served ball landing in the right half of the opponents' court.

Cross-court spike: A *spike* traveling diagonally from the *spiker* to the longest part of the opponents' court.

Cushioning: The action of absorbing the energy of a *spike* during a *dig*.

Decoy: An offensive play designed to disguise or mask the *spiker* who will actually receive the *set*.

Deep set: A ball placed by the *setter* designed to be hit well away from the net in order to confuse the *block*.

Dig: Passing a spiked ball or any ball dropping rapidly to the floor.

Dink: A legal push in which the fingers are used to move the ball over or around the blockers.

Dive: An attempt to save a low ball by stretching out to get under it.

Double block: Two players working in unison to intercept a spiked ball at or near the net.

Double hit: Successive contact between the ball and a player.

Double quick: Two hitters approaching the *setter* from both front and back for a quick inside set. The middle blocker must commit to blocking one or the other.

Doubles: A game with two players on a side. Doubles are usually played on the beach but may be played indoors as well.

Down ball: A ball played over the net by the opposing team that the blockers elect not to *block* because they judge the *spiker* not to be a threat or because the ball has been *set* far off the net.

Five-one: An offensive system using five hitters and one *setter*.

Five set: A ball placed by the *setter* to the right front hitter and opposite the direction the setter is facing. See *back set*.

Floater: A serve with no spin that follows an erratic path as it reaches the receiving team.

Forearm pass: A *bump pass*.

Foul: A violation as defined by the rules.

Four set: A ball placed by the *setter* one foot from the sideline and one to two feet above the net.

Four-two: An offensive system using four hitters and two *setters*.

Free ball: A ball that the blockers see will be returned by the opposition by any method other than a *spike*. When the blockers call "free ball!" the team should drop into serve-receive formation.

Head shot: Hitting a blocker in the head with the ball.

Held ball: An official's call that indicates a player has allowed the ball to come to rest during contact. It is a foul and terminates play.

Hit: To jump and strike the ball with an open hand and with a maximum of force.

Hot dog: An overly lucky or overly exuberant player.

Key: To discern a team's next offensive play by close observation of an individual's behavior before and leading to that play.

Line: The marks that distinguish the boundaries of a volleyball court.

Line serve: A *serve* made straight down the opponent's left sideline.

Line shot: A ball spiked along the opponent's sideline, closest to the hitter, and outside the *block*.

Maggot: Any member of an opposing team.

Maggot shot: A slow topspin shot that catches a player out of position and embarrasses him or her deeply.

Middle back: A defensive system that uses the middle back player to cover deep *spikes*.

Middle up: A defensive system that uses the middle back player to cover *dinks* or short shots.

Multiple offense: A system of play that relies on *sets* other than, but in addition to, outside regular sets. It may employ two or three hitters.

Netting: Contact by a player with the net while the ball is in play. Netting is a *foul* and ends play.

Off hand: The side of the court that is the same as a player's dominant hand; the right side of the court for right-handers, the left side of the court for left-handers.

Off-speed hit: A ball that loses impetus rapidly because it is deliberately struck with less than usual force.

One-arm dig: To play a spiked ball with the right or left forearm only; used when a *bump pass* cannot be used.

One set: A very quick, low *set* delivered one to two feet above the net and *hit* while the ball is still rising.

On hand: The side of the court that is the opposite of a player's dominant hand.

Out of bounds: A ball that (1) falls outside the side or end lines, (2) touches either of the *antennas* or the referee, (3) touches the net outside the boundary markers on the net, or (4) passes over the net not entirely within the antennas.

Overhand pass: A ball played with both hands open, controlled by the fingers, taken with the face below the ball, and passed in the direction the player is facing.

Overhand serve: Putting the ball in play by hitting it with the hand above the shoulder.

Pass: Any attempt to move the ball from one player to another. The *bump* and the *set* are types of passes.

Play set: Preconceived attacks called by the *setter* that attempt to create favorable spiking conditions and avoid the *block*.

Player in motion: Pulling a hitter from his or her usual position to another position to create a more advantageous offensive play.

Power alley or power lane: See *crosscourt spike*.

Rotation: The clockwise movement of a team's players to the next position following a *side-out*.

Seam: The intersecting area of coverage between two players.

Serve: The initial contact made by a player with the ball in order to begin play.

Set: A pass that places the ball where a hitter can *spike* it.

Setter: The specialized player whose responsibility it is to place the ball for an attack.

Shoot set: A ball placed by the *setter* one foot from the sideline and one to two feet above the net. Also referred to as a *four set*.

Short court: The 30-by-50-foot court used for playing doubles, as specified in the official rules. Noted more in its breach than in its observance.

Side-out: That change of service that occurs when the serving team has failed to score a point.

Six-pack: To hit an opposing player in the face, head, or chest with a *spike*.

Six set: A regular outside *set* placed by the *setter* about ten feet above the net, near the *antenna* the setter is facing. Also referred to simply as a *regular*.

Six-two: An offensive system that utilizes three hitters at the net and a *setter* coming from the back row. Four of the players are hitters only; two double as setters and hitters.

Slimes: The opposing team.

Soft block: An attempt to intercept a spiked ball and keep it in play on the blocker's side of the net.

Spike: To jump and *hit* the ball with an open hand and with a maximum of force.

Spiker: A player who attempts to force the ball to the floor of the opponents' court by hitting or dinking.

Stuff: To totally thwart a spike by *blocking* the ball.

Switch: To change the court positions of players after the *serve* in order to facilitate *setting*, *hitting*, or *blocking*.

Three set: A low *set* placed by the *setter* 10 feet from the left sideline, usually for the outside hitter.

Thrown ball: An official's call that indicates a player has allowed the ball to come to rest during contact. It is a *foul* and terminates play.

Turning in: The action of the end blocker to turn his or her outside hand in toward the court to prevent the *spiker* from deliberately hitting the ball into the *block* and out of bounds.

Two set: A low *set* placed by the *setter* two to four feet above the net, usually for the middle hitter.

Underhand serve: To put the ball in play by striking it with the hand below the shoulder.

Wipe shot: A *spiker's* conscious effort to hit the ball off the blocker's hands and out of bounds.

INDEX